The Catholic Biblical School Program

YEAR THREE

OLD TESTAMENT CONTINUED: EXILE AND RESTORATION

STUDENT WORKBOOK

Prepared by
Angelo G. Giuliano, Judith A. Hubert, Dorothy Jonaitis, and Brian Schmisek

PAULIST PRESS
New York/Mahwah, NJ

Acknowledgements

The Publisher gratefully acknowledges use of the following materials: "Classical Prophets: Differentia from Early Prophets," by Joseph Jensen, OSB, from *Ethical Dimensions of the Prophets*, copyright © 2006 by Liturgical Press; "The Prism of Sennacherib" from *Ancient Near Eastern Texts*, edited by James B. Pritchard, copyright © 1969 by Princeton University Press; "The Meaning of Exile" by Eloi LeClerc, OFM, from *People of God in the Night*, copyright © 1976 by Franciscan Press; "David, the King: Two Biblical Portraits," by Leslie J. Hoppe, OFM, reprinted from *The Bible Today* 42, 3 (2004); "Outline of Psalms According to Literary Form," by Carroll Stuhlmueller, CP, from *Psalms I (Psalms 1–72)* (Old Testament Message Series), copyright © 1983 by Liturgical Press.

Special thanks to Mary E. Ingenthron for the biblical drawings that are included throughout this book.

The scripture quotations contained herein are from the New Revised Standard Version: Catholic Edition Copyright © 1989 and 1993, by the Division of Christian Education of the National Council of the Churches of Christ in the United States of America. Used by permission. All rights reserved.

Cover design by Sharyn Banks

Book design by Celine Allen

Nihil Obstat: Rev. Msgr. Robert Coerver
                  Censor Librorum

Imprimatur: + Most Reverend Kevin J. Farrell
                  Bishop of Dallas

December 29, 2008

The *Nihil Obstat* and *Imprimatur* are official declarations that the work contains nothing contrary to Faith and Morals. It is not implied thereby that those granting the *Nihil Obstat* and *Imprimatur* agree with the contents, statements, or opinions expressed.

ISBN 978-0-8091-9588-6

Published by Paulist Press
997 Macarthur Boulevard
Mahwah, New Jersey 07430

www.paulistpress.com

Printed and bound in the
United States of America

Dedication

It is with respect and gratitude that this revision of *The Denver Catholic Biblical School Program* is dedicated to Sister Macrina Scott, OSF. It was her recognition of the need for a serious Bible study for the Catholic laity that led to the creation of the Catholic Biblical School in 1982. As the founder and for twenty years director of the school, Sister Macrina is a leader in the area of adult Catholic biblical literacy. We are grateful to her for the great gift that she has given to the church.

Because of her vision and determination, literally thousands of Catholics have had their eyes and hearts opened to the word and have grown in faith and knowledge, deepening their relationship with God through their study of scripture. With the publication of the Biblical School materials by Paulist Press beginning in 1994, Sister Macrina's dream bore fruit throughout the country. It is our hope that these revisions, renamed *The Catholic Biblical School Program*, will keep that dream alive well into the twenty-first century.

In addition, we would be remiss not to acknowledge the significant contributions of Steve Mueller, PhD, to the development of the original Biblical School program. We also remember Mary E. Ingenthron, now deceased, whose delightful illustrations grace this book.

Contents

SUPPLEMENTARY READINGS

Foreword

Welcome to the Catholic Biblical School Program. In the Catholic Church, sacred scripture is often called "the soul of theology." The study of sacred scripture on the part of Catholics reached new levels after Vatican II. Many programs have arisen to meet that need. One was the Denver Catholic Biblical School, which was founded more than twenty-five years ago. Since that time, the program has flourished in many places throughout the United States and beyond. One reason for its success is that it incorporates the fruit of the "indispensable method" of historical criticism into the rich faith tradition of the church and the lives of the students.

As dean of the University of Dallas School of Ministry, I was elated when we were able to hire first Mr. Gene Giuliano; then Sr. Dorothy Jonaitis, OP; and finally Ms. Angeline Hubert. Each of them is an acknowledged author of the "original" Denver Catholic Biblical School program materials, and each of them taught in the school for a time. Now, as faculty members at the Catholic Biblical School of the School of Ministry, they bring significant experience to their writing.

In this revision, we have incorporated lessons learned from scholarship, from classroom teaching (our own and others'), from updated materials, including the publication of the *Catechism of the Catholic Church* and statements from the Pontifical Biblical Commission, and our own growth in spirituality and faith. We present the product of countless hours of discussion, prayer, and scholarly debate.

By using this workbook, you will become more familiar with the Bible. You will learn about its stories, its characters, its places, its themes, its promises, and its hopes. This sacred text will meet you in your own life, with your cares, concerns, worries, hopes, ambitions, and faith. The sacred is something that exhausts us. We do not exhaust it. Time and again we approach it anew, whether we are seventeen or seventy-seven. We encourage you on your path to learning more about the sacred text, its inspired character, and its primary author. We hope you will find the workbook material nourishing both academically and spiritually.

Brian Schmisek, PhD
Dean, School of Ministry
University of Dallas

Introduction

Welcome to your third year of the Catholic Biblical School Program, *Old Testament Continued: Exile and Restoration*. After completing the first-year journey from Genesis through Kings and the second-year journey with Jesus and the early Christian community, you are a seasoned traveler. You are ready to take up the study of the Hebrew prophets, the psalms, and other literature of the exile and restoration.

A Preview of the Third-Year Journey

This year we return to the experience of the Hebrew people. In particular we trace the historical events of the tumultuous time from about 750 to 400 BC. We study the destruction of the Northern Kingdom of Israel in 722/21 BC, the destruction of the Southern Kingdom of Judah in 587/586 BC, the exile in Babylon, and finally the restoration of the people to the land after the exile. In the midst of these crucial events, the prophets spoke God's word of judgment and hope to the people. They reminded them that God was at work in the everyday social, political, and religious crises that they faced.

In the first unit, we concentrate on the great prophets who exercised their ministry prior to the exile. We begin with Amos and Hosea, prophets to the Northern Kingdom. Then we shift our focus to Isaiah of Jerusalem, Micah, Zephaniah, Nahum, and the incomparable Jeremiah, prophets to the Southern Kingdom. With the threat of destruction and annihilation facing the people, these prophets challenged them to see their lives from God's perspective.

In the second unit, we focus first on the exile. After experiencing the pain of the destruction of Jerusalem in the Book of Lamentations and Obadiah's indictment of Edom, we concentrate on the two great prophets of the exile, Ezekiel and Second Isaiah (Deutero-Isaiah). These two men recognized in the midst of the utter hopelessness of their situation an experience of God's saving presence. They re-thought the theology of the LORD and his relationship to his people in new and creative ways. We also study Haggai and Zechariah who urged the rebuilding of the temple and Third Isaiah who was active during the early post-exilic period. Finally, we explore the restoration of the land under the priest Ezra and the governor Nehemiah.

In the third unit, we continue to study the restoration era. 1 and 2 Chronicles exemplify how the Jews rewrote their history to meet the needs of the post-exilic community. The prophets Joel, Malachi, and Deutero-Zechariah offer further insights into the restoration period. The beautiful Book of Ruth inspires us with its message of courage, fidelity, and tolerance toward outsiders. Finally, we turn to a study of the poetic love lyrics in the Song of Solomon (Song of Songs) and the magnificent psalms that express so eloquently the prayer life of Israel.

Our third year will be a journey to the center of the Hebrew faith experience: the disaster of exile and the unexpected joy of restoration that formed Judaism. Just as we Christians perceive our faith in light of the death and resurrection of Jesus, so Judaism perceived its faith in light of the exile and restoration, which played a significant role in shaping the way that Judaism understood itself.

We will also be reminded of how important the prophets were for the early Christians, who scrutinized the scriptures for clues to the meaning of Jesus. Christians found in the prophetic texts insights into Jesus' identity and into the meaning of his death and resurrection. The New Testament books that you studied last year were full of quotations and allusions to the prophets. As you familiarize yourself with the prophets' words and message, follow the cross-references to the New Testament to discover how these passages were used by New Testament authors.

Preparing for the Third-Year Journey

As you know, the most important resource for your study is your Bible. The translations recommended in your first year, the *New American Bible* (NAB), the *Revised Standard Version* (RSV) or the *New Revised Standard Version* (NRSV), and the *New Jerusalem Bible* (NJB) are all good choices. Using more than one translation can be helpful, but be warned that there are occasionally variations of chapter and verse numbers in some of the books that you will be studying this year. The division of the biblical books into chapters and verses was done long after the text was written. There is nothing divinely inspired about these designations. Our primary chapter and verse numbers are those of the *New Revised Standard Version*. Chapter and verse numbers for the *New American Bible* and the *New Jerusalem Bible* are given in parentheses when they differ from those in the NRSV.

Once again, we encourage you to reread Vatican II's Dogmatic Constitution on Divine Revelation (*Dei Verbum*) to review the principles and norms of the Catholic Church's teaching on the nature, transmission, interpretation, and application of divine revelation. You will also find paragraphs 50–184 of the *Catechism of the Catholic Church* helpful for refreshing your understanding of God's revelation and our response of faith. As in the first two years of your study, we have suggested readings from the *Catechism* in the **Further Reading** section of each lesson.

As you read various commentaries and listen to lectures, keep in mind that there is a range of opinions among biblical scholars about such matters as literary genres, authorship, and dating of biblical writings. Time does not permit the exploration of all the various hypotheses. This workbook and the assigned readings try to present the current scholarly consensus on given questions, but we realize that alternate views are held by other reputable scholars. Since scholarly research on the Bible is always developing, we know that these positions are subject to further revision. Focus primarily on learning to read and interpret the Bible "according to the same Spirit by whom it was written" (*Dei Verbum*, §12). Learn to apply it to your life "within the living tradition of the Church, whose first concern is fidelity to the revelation attested by the Bible" (Pontifical Biblical Commission, *The Interpretation of the Bible in the Church*, [1993], III).

Once again you will be using your Eerdmans *Dictionary of the Bible* for background materials that will clarify the biblical texts and your Hammond *Atlas of the Bible Lands* that will help you find the locations of the people and events that you study this year.

For each unit of study, we will also recommend textbooks that we have found helpful for understanding the Old Testament material. In particular, Lawrence Boadt's *Reading the Old Testament*, which you used in the first year of our program, Thomas L. Leclerc's *Introduction to the Prophets*, and the Collegeville Commentary on *Ezekiel, Daniel*, will help you with your studies this year. We also recommend the classic study, *The Prophets*, by Rabbi Abraham Heschel. Not only are his insights extraordinary but we think it is valuable to see and understand the prophets the way a Jewish scholar does.

Much has been written about the Old Testament prophets in the last twenty-five years. We have listed many books and articles in the **Further Reading** section of each lesson. You may also check what is available through your parish or public library or any other libraries to which you have access.

Making the Journey

You are already familiar with the process of making the biblical journey using our study materials. The **Geography Task** helps you situate major events in the lives of the prophets and the people of Israel in their geographic setting. The **Important**

Terms focus your attention on the key concepts emphasized in each lesson. The **Written Work** leads you directly to the Bible texts that you have been assigned to read and helps you apply these texts to your life.

More than any other part of the Old Testament, the prophets' message is intimately connected to the social and political situation of their times. You will need to increase your awareness of the historical times and customs of the Jewish people in order to appreciate the meaning of the prophets' words and actions. Since you are reading and studying for more than mere information, your involvement with this material will stimulate changes in your thinking and your actions.

This year one of the **Exercises** found after the written work will focus on the creation of a time line, which you will build as the year progresses. This time line will help you situate the kings, prophets, and other significant people and events you meet in the biblical text in their historical context. Each week we also provide **Optional Challenges** that require a bit more thinking and research than the basic questions. You may also find other intriguing things that you want to explore. Make these into optional challenges and share your findings with your group.

Each lesson also includes a **Memory Verse Suggestion**. You might think that memorizing these and other verses of scripture is irrelevant but these verses are a first step in making the Bible texts your own. Without some memorization, it is difficult to have scripture texts readily available for your prayer and application to the situations of your life. You will find that there are many profound and helpful verses from the prophets that you will want to make your own. Some of these verses are among the most familiar and most popular in the entire Old Testament.

Companions for the Journey

As you have learned from your work during previous years in the program, there is not only one teacher in the class. As adult learners you know that some of your best teachers are the people in your small group with whom you share your journey. Again this year, they will surprise you with their insights into the prophets and their message. Just as each of the classical prophets takes a particular perspective that depends on his own experiences and circumstances, so each one in your group will have his or her special viewpoint on the material you study each week. God's word can be found and heard not just as it is encapsulated in the scripture text, but also as it is incarnated in the persons with whom you study. As always, your group sharing should be guided by:

The Ten Commandments of Group Process

1. Work to build trust and intimacy within your group.

2. Get to the heart of the passage. Don't just skim the surface.

3. Give everyone in your group a chance to talk. No speeches!

4. Speak connectedly with previous speakers. Consciously work at building bridges with what has already been said.

5. While one person speaks, everyone else listens.

6. Never ridicule or cut down another's answers.

7. When you disagree, do so with respect.

8. Do not fear silence.

9. If you have not completed your homework, be a participant "listener" for those questions that you have not completed.

10. Enjoy yourself!

As you have discovered from the previous two years, the journey brings many surprises. Students often begin their study of the prophets with a vague awareness of the meaning of biblical prophecy and the role that the prophets played in the religious experience of Israel. As their study progresses, many students are surprised that aspects of a prophet's situation are similar to their own situation. Consequently, the message of the prophets is not experienced as having relevance for the prophets' time only. Rather, the challenge of God's word as the prophets experienced it in their situations once again comes alive as you study the prophets. As Amos put it so well,

> The lion has roared;
>   who will not fear?
> The Lord GOD has spoken;
>   who can but prophesy?
>   (Amos 3:8; NRSV)

UNIT I
Prophecy Before the Exile

After completing this unit, you will be able to:

1. Describe the historical and social situation in Israel from the eighth century BC to the fall of Jerusalem in 587/86 BC.

2. Explain the basic forms of prophetic speech and the methods by which the prophetic message was handed on.

3. Recognize the prophetic themes of vocation (call), covenant fidelity, social justice, the marriage of God and Israel, and the destruction of the temple.

4. Appropriate and apply the Old Testament prophetic mission and message to contemporary issues.

Textbooks

Primary Text: The Bible. Use a good translation with scholarly notes.

Other Texts: For helpful background and handy reference we recommend:
Eerdmans *Dictionary of the Bible* (cited as EDB)
Hammond's *Atlas of the Bible Lands* (cited as Hammond Atlas)
Lawrence Boadt's *Reading the Old Testament* (cited as Boadt)
Abraham Heschel's *The Prophets* (cited as Heschel)
Thomas L. Leclerc's *Introduction to the Prophets* (cited as Leclerc)

Assignments

Each lesson is to be studied in preparation for your group discussion. For each biblical passage, study the biblical text and footnotes for that particular passage, complete other assigned readings, and do the written work *on a separate page.*

I.1   INTRODUCTION TO THE PROPHETS IN ISRAEL

I.2   AMOS

I.3   HOSEA

I.4   ISAIAH 1–12

I.5   ISAIAH 25, 28–39

I.6   MICAH, ZEPHANIAH, NAHUM

I.7   JEREMIAH 1–6

I.8   JEREMIAH 7–20

I.9   JEREMIAH 21–24, 26–33, 36–38, 52

I.10   UNIT ONE REVIEW

Introduction to the Prophets in Israel

> **After studying this lesson, you will be able to:**
> 1. Understand the historical and social factors that contributed to the development of prophecy in Israel.
> 2. Recall the early prophets covered in the narrative material of the Books of Samuel and Kings studied in the first year of the Catholic Biblical School Program.
> 3. Recognize the differences between the early prophets and the classical prophets.
> 4. Describe the characteristics of biblical prophecy.

Read

Boadt, pages 303–15; Heschel, pages xiii–31; "Classical Prophets: Differentia from Early Prophets," #1 in the SUPPLEMENTARY READINGS at the back of this workbook

Geography Task

Using the map on page 21 in your Hammond Atlas, locate Israel (the Northern Kingdom) and Judah (the Southern Kingdom). Note the size of each kingdom, the topography, and the major cities.

Important Terms

Prophet, early/former prophets, classical/latter prophets

Written Work

1. Based on the reading assignment,
   a. Describe the role of the biblical prophet.
   b. Compare and contrast the early/former prophets with the classical/latter prophets.

2. Based on your study of Joshua through 2 Kings (Deuteronomistic History) in the first year, select one of the early prophets and describe how that individual exercised the role of prophet. Cite references.

3. In the middle of a crisis, it is not always easy to distinguish between false prophets and true prophets. Using the story in 2 Kings 18:13—19:7, imagine that you were living in the city of Jerusalem when it was under siege by the Assyrians.
   a. What reasons would you have for believing Isaiah?
   b. What reasons would you have for believing the Rabshakeh?

4. Heschel states that "the prophets remind us of the moral state of a people: Few are guilty, but all are responsible."
   a. What do you think he means?
   b. Describe a contemporary example of his assertion.

5. According to Heschel, how does the prophet experience God?

Exercise

(Note that this is part of the required study but does not always involve a written response.) As you work your way through the unit, choose a verse that you will memorize so that you are able to write it out with the proper citation (translation used and reference [book, chapter, and verse]). Suggestions are given for each lesson, but you may choose another verse that you like.

ADDITIONAL SUGGESTIONS FOR THE STUDENT

Optional Challenges

1. a. Name some "prophet(s)" of today.
   b. In what ways are their roles similar to that of the biblical prophets as described in your response to the first question under "Written Work" above?
   c. What do you need to hear from each of the "prophets" you named? Be specific.
2. How do the prophets Elijah and Elisha serve as role models for Luke's portrayal of Jesus as a prophet? Cite references from the Old and New Testaments.

Memory Verse Suggestion

[Moses said to Joshua] "Are you jealous for my sake? Would that all the LORD's people were prophets, and that the LORD would put his spirit on them!" (Numbers 11:29; NRSV)

Further Reading

Catechism of the Catholic Church, §64, §218, and §2584.

Walter Brueggemann, *An Introduction to the Old Testament: the Canon and Christian Imagination* (Louisville: Westminster John Knox Press, 2003), 101–8.

Thomas L. Leclerc, *Introduction to the Prophets: Their Stories, Sayings and Scrolls* (New York/Mahwah, NJ: Paulist Press, 2007), 61–99.

Bruce V. Malchow, *Social Justice in the Hebrew Bible: What Is New and What Is Old* (Collegeville, MN: The Liturgical Press, 1996), 31–48.

Thomas W. Overholt, "Prophet, Prophecy," in Eerdmans *Dictionary of the Bible*, ed. David Noel Freedman (Grand Rapids: William B. Eerdmans Publishing Company, 2000), 1086–88.

here come the ecstatic prophets! confess—wouldn't you rather read about them than run into them?

I.2
Amos

After studying this lesson, you will be able to:

1. Identify in their historical and social context the person and message of Amos.

2. Better understand Amos's emphasis on the obligations of covenant life, in particular as they relate to social justice.

Read   Amos 1–9; Heschel, pages 32–46; Leclerc, pages 123–41; "Pre-exilic Prophets: Overview—Amos," #2 in the SUPPLEMENTARY READINGS at the back of this workbook

Geography Task   Using the map on page 21 in your Hammond Atlas, locate Tekoa and the areas condemned in the woes of Amos 1–2.

Important Terms   Justice, oracles against the nations

Written Work

1. a. In what ways does Amos describe God for his hearers? Cite references.
    b. Do you think Amos' description of God is effective? Why or why not?

2. a. What sins are condemned in Amos 5:10–12 and 8:4–6?
    b. In what ways are these sins a violation of the covenant? Be specific.

3. a. What do you learn about Amos himself from chapter 7? Cite references.
    b. How does this description relate to *your idea* of a prophet prior to your study this year?

4. The classical prophets often refer to the exodus/wilderness experiences of the Israelites. For what reasons does Amos refer to these experiences in:
    a. Amos 2:10?
    b. Amos 4:10?
    c. Amos 5:25?

5. What does Amos reveal about God's dealings with non-Israelite nations in Amos 1–2 and 9:7?

6. How are you challenged by the prophet Amos? Be specific.

Exercise   Begin constructing a time-line of kings and prophets that will be helpful to you for your study, review, and possibly even later teaching. Add to it each week, updating it for each of the prophets you study.

ADDITIONAL SUGGESTIONS FOR THE STUDENT

Optional Challenges

1. In the style of Amos 4:1 and 6:4–6, describe those today who profit at the expense of the poor.
2. Write a report on the preaching of Amos that the authorities might have given to the king of Israel.
3. Amos 9:11–15 was probably added by a later editor who lived after both Samaria and Jerusalem had been conquered. What differences do you find between this section and the rest of Amos? Be specific.

Memory Verse Suggestion

The time is surely coming, says the Lord GOD, when I will send a famine on the land; not a famine of bread, or a thirst for water, but of hearing the words of the LORD. (Amos 8:11; NRSV)

Further Reading

Catechism of the Catholic Church, §2409.

Walter Brueggemann, *An Introduction to the Old Testament: The Canon and Christian Imagination* (Louisville: Westminster John Knox Press, 2003), 223–28.

Abraham Heschel, *The Prophets* (New York: Harper & Row, 1962, as revised by Susannah Heschel [Perennial Classics, 2001]), 358–68.

Leslie Hoppe, OFM, *There Shall Be No Poor Among You: Poverty in the Bible* (Nashville: Abingdon Press, 2004), 68–72.

Joseph Jensen, OSB, *Ethical Dimensions of the Prophets* (Collegeville, MN: Liturgical Press, 2006), 67–91.

Michelle Tooley, "Just, Justice," in Eerdmans *Dictionary of the Bible*, ed. David Noel Freedman (Grand Rapids: William B. Eerdmans Publishing Company, 2000), 448–51.

Amos 1:2 "Yahweh roars from Zion"

1.3
Hosea

After studying this lesson, you will be able to:

1. Describe in their historical and social context the person and message of Hosea.

2. Recognize the major themes of the Book of Hosea, especially the analogy of the covenant with marriage.

Read

Hosea 1–6, 11–14; Heschel, pages 47–50, 53–58, 70–75; Leclerc, pages 142–61; "Pre-exilic Prophets: Overview—Hosea," #2 in the SUPPLEMENTARY READINGS at the back of this workbook

Geography Task

Using the map on page 21 in your Hammond Atlas, locate Bethel, Gilgal, Gilead, Mizpah, Ramah, and Shechem. Using the map on page 17 in your Hammond Atlas, locate Moresheth-Gath.

Important Terms

Covenant fidelity, Israel as unfaithful wife

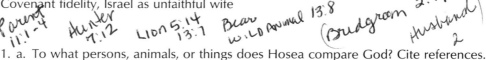

Parent 11:1-4   Hunter 7:12   Lion 5:14 13:7   Bear 13:8 wild animal   (Bridegroom 2:19 Husband) 2

Written Work

Falconer 11:10-11

1. a. To what persons, animals, or things does Hosea compare God? Cite references.
   b. What particular feelings (e.g., anger) does God have? Cite references.
   c. Describe God as you think Hosea understood God. Be specific.

2. Some people say that the God of the Old Testament is a God of justice whereas the God of the New Testament is a God of love.
   a. Cite two specific texts in Hosea that support the understanding of God as a God of justice.
   b. Cite two specific texts in Hosea that support the understanding of God as a God of love. _2:19-20   2:14-15_
   c. Do you think that these two understandings of God are incompatible? Why or why not?

3. Hosea refers to the exodus/wilderness experience in 2:14–15 (2:16–17 NAB and NJB), 12:9–13 (12:10–14 NAB and NJB), and 13:4–6. According to Hosea, what was Israel's experience of God in the exodus/wilderness? _Pg 155-6_

4. Read Hosea 6:1–3.
   a. To what do you think Hosea is referring in 6:2?
   b. In 1 Corinthians 15:3–4, do you think that Paul has Hosea 6:1–3 in mind? Why or why not?

5. Hosea 11:1–8 images God as a parent.
   a. Briefly summarize Hosea's description.
   b. In what ways have you experienced God as a loving parent?

6. Which passages in Hosea can you relate to your spiritual journey? Explain.

Exercise   Us̶
assignm̶

ADDITIONAL SUGGESTIONS FOR T̶

Optional
Challenges
1. Express the message of Hosea in an o̶
2. Write a report that the king's secret police̶
3. How would you describe Jeroboam II, during w̶
   2 Kings 14:23–29 and Amos 7:9–14 for help.
4. Compare Hosea 1:4–6 with 2 Kings 9–10. How do you ex̶
   Elisha's and Hosea's attitudes toward Jehu?

Memory
Verse
Suggestions
Therefore, I will now allure her, and bring her into the wilderness, and speak te̶
(Hosea 2:14; NRSV)

Yet it was I who taught Ephraim to walk, I took them up in my arms; but they did not know
that I healed them. I led them with cords of human kindness, with bands of love. I was to
them like those who lift infants to their cheeks. I bent down to them and fed them. (Hosea
11:3–4; NRSV)

Further
Reading
Catechism of the Catholic Church, §208, §370, §1611, and §2100.
Walter Brueggemann, *An Introduction to the Old Testament: The Canon and Christian
   Imagination* (Louisville: Westminster John Knox Press, 2003), 214–19.
Carol J. Dempsey, OP, "Hosea's Use of Nature," *The Bible Today* 39, 6 (2001): 347–53.
J. Edward Owens, OSST, "Reflections on Hosea 11," *The Bible Today* 39, 6 (2001): 343–46.
Gregory J. Polan, OSB, "Hosea's Interpretation of Israel's Traditions," *The Bible Today* 39, 6
   (2001): 329–34.
Gregory Vall, "Hosea and 'Knowledge of God,'" *The Bible Today* 39, 6 (2001): 335–41.

Hosea 11:4 "I was like someone lifting an infant"

al Davidic

ۍ2–74; "Pre-Exilic Prophets:
:d *Scriptures in the Christian*
ɔack of this workbook

ɔcate Syria and note the extent of

holiness, Immanuel/Emmanuel,

**Written
Work**

the worship offered by the people?
ɔrship today? Why or why not?

2. a. In Isɔ͜   ͜iah envision a peaceful world?
   b. Describe ͵   ͜aceful world.

3. a. What do you learɔ   ͜ɔt God from Isaiah's vision (Isa 6:1–10)? Cite references.
   b. Where does the church use Isaiah 6:3 in the eucharistic liturgy?
   c. Why do you think that the church uses it at that point in the liturgy?

4. a. In Isaiah 7:10–17, about whom in his immediate historical context is the prophet
      speaking?
   b. Explain how Matthew sees this prophecy in a new light.

5. a. Why do you think that the Lectionary uses Isaiah 8:23—9:6 (9:1–7 in the NRSV) at the
      Christmas Midnight Mass?
   b. How does this text enrich your experience of the Incarnation?

6. Isaiah 11:1–10 has been understood by the church in a messianic context.
   a. What characteristics of the messiah himself do you find in this passage?
   b. What characteristics of the reign of the messiah do you find in this passage?

Exercise

Using the material in Isaiah 1–12, add to the time-line of kings and prophets that you began
in assignment I.2.

ADDITIONAL SUGGESTIONS FOR THE STUDENT

Optional Challenges

1. Express in an original artistic or poetic form one or more of the images used in Isaiah 1–12.
2. Bring to class your favorite creative expressions (literary, visual, or musical) of a text from Isaiah 1–12. Write an explanation of why you chose this creative work and share it with your group.

Memory Verse Suggestion

The spirit of the LORD shall rest on him, the spirit of wisdom and understanding, the spirit of counsel and might, the spirit of knowledge and the fear of the LORD. (Isaiah 11:2; NRSV)

Further Reading

Catechism of the Catholic Church, §497, §712, §1831, and §2304–2305.

Patrick T. Cronauer, OSB, "Reading First Isaiah in Context," *The Bible Today* 43, 6 (2005): 341–47.

Leslie Hoppe, OFM, *There Shall Be No Poor Among You: Poverty in the Bible* (Nashville: Abingdon Press, 2004), 72–75.

David B. Howell, "Immanuel," in Eerdmans *Dictionary of the Bible*, ed. David Noel Freedman (Grand Rapids: William B. Eerdmans Publishing Company, 2000), 633–34.

Thomas L. Leclerc, MS, "Isaiah and the God of Justice," *The Bible Today* 43, 6 (2005): 359–64.

Elizabeth M. Nagel, "The Ideal Leader in the Kingdom of God," *The Bible Today* 43, 6 (2005): 353–58.

Aaron W. Park, "Zion," in Eerdmans *Dictionary of the Bible*, ed. David Noel Freedman (Grand Rapids: William B. Eerdmans Publishing Company, 2000), 1421–22.

Gregory J. Polan, OSB, "The Call and Commission of Isaiah," *The Bible Today* 43, 6 (2005): 348–52.

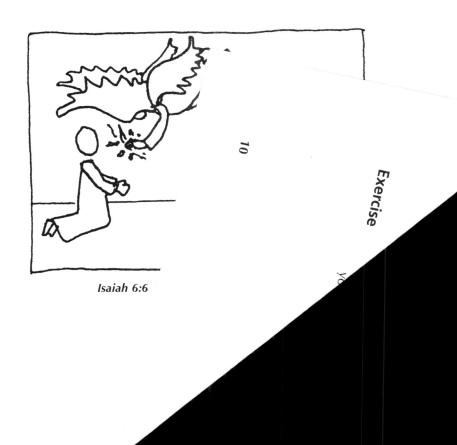

Isaiah 6:6

Isaiah 25, 28–39

After studying this lesson, you will be able to:

1. Describe more fully in their historical and social context the person and message of Isaiah.

2. Recognize major themes from the Book of Isaiah, especially his understanding of trust in God and the idea of the remnant of Israel (Isa 37:31–32).

3. Describe the siege of Jerusalem by the Assyrian King Sennacherib in 701 BC and contrast the biblical interpretation of this event with that given by the Assyrians.

Read

Isaiah 25, 28–39; Heschel, pages 94–112; Leclerc, pages 174–87; "The Prism of Sennacherib, iii 18–49," #4 in the SUPPLEMENTARY READINGS at the back of this workbook

Geography Task

Using the map on page 22 of your Hammond Atlas, locate Babylon, Egypt, Jerusalem, and Nineveh. Using another source, locate the modern country in which Babylon and Nineveh are located.

Syria

Important Terms

Prism of Sennacherib, remnant

Written Work

1. Apocalyptic literature is intended to give hope and comfort to those in crisis. What examples of hope and comfort do you find in Isaiah 25? Cite references.

2. a. To what animals is God compared in Isaiah 31? Cite references.
   b. What do these comparisons reveal about God? Be specific.
   c. Do these images contribute to your understanding of God? Why or why not?

3. Isaiah 35:1–6, 10 is used in the Lectionary for the third Sunday of Advent in Cycle A. Why do you think that this text was chosen?

4. Isaiah 36–37, 2 Kings 18:13—19:37, and the Prism of Sennacherib (see SUPPLEMENTARY READING #4) all describe the siege of Jerusalem.
   a. How do these texts differ in their description of the event? Be specific.
   b. Why do you think that the accounts differ? Explain.

5. a. According to Isaiah 38, how does Hezekiah describe life after death?
   b. Briefly explain how Hezekiah's thoughts about death resonate with thoughts or feelings that you have had about death.

Using the material in Isaiah 25 and 28–39, add to the time-line of kings and prophets that you began in assignment I.2.

ADDITIONAL SUGGESTIONS FOR THE STUDENT

Optional Challenges

1. a. Compile a list of passages from Isaiah 1–39 that stress:
      i. God's holiness.
      ii. Israel as the remnant.
   b. Based on these passages, what is your understanding of God's holiness and Israel as the remnant?
2. Express in an original prayer or artistic form a passage from Isaiah 25, 28–39.

Memory Verse Suggestion

For thus said the Lord GOD, the Holy One of Israel: In returning and rest you shall be saved; in quietness and in trust shall be your strength. (Isaiah 30:15; NRSV)

Further Reading

Catechism of the Catholic Church, §368 and §1502.
Joseph Jensen, OSB, *Ethical Dimensions of the Prophets* (Collegeville, MN: Liturgical Press, 2006), 110–28.
Dorothy Jonaitis, OP, *Unmasking Apocalyptic Texts* (New York/Mahwah, NJ: Paulist Press, 2005), 66–73.

Isaiah 28:5
"That day Yahweh Sabaoth will be a crown of splendor"

Why was Judah in "chief enemy" in the Assyrian Campaign?

I.6
Micah, Zephaniah, Nahum

After studying this lesson, you will be able to:

1. Set in their historical, political, and social contexts the persons and prophetic messages of Micah, Zephaniah, and Nahum.

2. Recognize the major themes and theological contributions of Micah, Zephaniah, and Nahum.

Read
Micah, Zephaniah, Nahum; Heschel, pages 124–29; Leclerc, pages 188–204, 212–26; ✓
"Pre-exilic Prophets: Overview—Micah, Zephaniah, Nahum," #2 in the SUPPLEMENTARY READINGS at the back of this workbook

Geography Task
Using the maps on pages 21 and 22 in your Hammond Atlas, locate the places condemned in Zephaniah 2:1–4, 8–15.

Important Terms
Covenant lawsuit, Day of the LORD

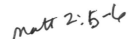
matt 2:5-6

Written Work
1. a. Where is Micah 5:2 (5:1 NAB and NJB) quoted in the New Testament?
   b. Because of its previous history, what special significance would Bethlehem have had for Micah?

2. Briefly explain how Micah 6:6–8 could be applied in our time.

3. a. What categories of leaders does Zephaniah condemn in chapter 3?
   b. For what are the leaders condemned?

4. Zephaniah 3:14–18 is used as the first reading for the third Sunday of Advent in Cycle C. Why do you think this text was chosen for the Advent season? Be specific.

5. According to EDB, "The book of Nahum has been regarded as an example of self-serving, nationalistic prophecy."
   a. How would you support this description with quotes from the Book of Nahum? Be specific.
   b. How could the Book of Nahum be described as good news?

6. Micah, Zephaniah, and Nahum see God's activity in the political and natural catastrophes of their time. Do you think such applications are appropriate today? Why or why not?

Exercises
1. Using the material in Micah, Zephaniah, and Nahum, add to the time-line of kings and prophets that you began in assignment I.2.
2. Review your grasp of the basic information covered so far by taking the "Self-Quiz: Mid-Unit One," #5 in the SUPPLEMENTARY READINGS at the back of this workbook.

ADDITIONAL SUGGESTIONS FOR THE STUDENT

Optional Challenges

1. Compose additional verses to continue God's words in Micah 6:3–4.
2. Express the promises of Zephaniah 3:9–20 in an original artistic or poetic form.
3. Bring to class examples of your favorite artistic expressions (literary, visual, or musical) of the Day of the LORD. Write an explanation of why you chose this creative work and share the explanation with your group.

Memory Verse Suggestions

He has told you, O mortal, what is good; and what does the LORD require of you but to do justice, and to love kindness, and to walk humbly with your God? (Micah 6:8; NRSV)

Sing aloud, O daughter Zion; shout, O Israel! Rejoice and exult with all your heart, O daughter Jerusalem! (Zephaniah 3:14; NRSV)

The LORD is slow to anger but great in power, and the LORD will by no means clear the guilty. His way is in whirlwind and storm, and the clouds are the dust of his feet. (Nahum 1:3; NRSV)

Further Reading

Catechism of the Catholic Church, §711, §716, and §762.

Walter Brueggemann, *An Introduction to the Old Testament: The Canon and Christian Imagination* (Louisville: Westminster John Knox Press, 2003), 233–40, 244–47.

Leslie Hoppe, OFM, *There Shall Be No Poor Among You: Poverty in the Bible* (Nashville: Abingdon Press, 2004), 75–85.

Greg A. King, "Day of the Lord," in Eerdmans *Dictionary of the Bible*, ed. David Noel Freedman (Grand Rapids: William B. Eerdmans Publishing Company, 2000), 324–25.

Daniel L. Smith-Christopher, "Of Swords and Plowshares: On Peace and the Hebrew Prophets," *The Bible Today* 46, 3 (2008): 155–59.

Micah 1:6 "So I shall make Samaria a ruin"

I.7
Jeremiah 1–6

> **After studying this lesson, you will be able to:**
> 1. Describe in their social, political, and historical contexts the person and message of the prophet Jeremiah.
> 2. Recognize the importance of Jeremiah's call and early oracles in understanding his prophetic work.
> 3. Characterize the poetic style and imagery used by Jeremiah.

Read
Jeremiah 1–6; Heschel, pages 130–40; Leclerc, pages 235–42, 251–55; "Pre-exilic Prophets: Overview—Jeremiah," #2 in the SUPPLEMENTARY READINGS at the back of this workbook

Geography Task
Using the map on page 25 of your Hammond Atlas, locate Anathoth.

Important Terms
Circumcision, idolatry

Written Work

1. a. What do you learn about Jeremiah's mission from the call story in Jeremiah 1:4–10? Be specific.
   b. If, like Jeremiah, you were to be called by God, what excuses might you use not to respond?

2. a. In Jeremiah 2:1—3:25, what images does Jeremiah use for idolatry?
   b. Do you think these images are effective? Why or why not?

3. Imagine that you are a resident of Jerusalem living at the time of Jeremiah. How would you respond to Jeremiah's vision (Jer 3:14–18) of a restoration that does not include the Ark of the Covenant?

4. a. Read Jeremiah 4:4; Deuteronomy 10:16, 30:6; Colossians 2:11; and Romans 2:25–29. Summarize what the ritual of circumcision symbolizes in these passages.
   b. What metaphor or ritual symbol would you use today to make the same point?

5. Which passages from Jeremiah 1–6 can you relate to your spiritual journey? Why?

Exercises

1. Using the material in Jeremiah 1–6, add to the time-line of kings and prophets that you began in assignment I.2.
2. Read Jeremiah 3:1–5 and 3:19—4:4 together. Can you see that this may have originally been one poem that was interrupted by other material in the final editing of the text as we now have it?

ADDITIONAL SUGGESTIONS FOR THE STUDENT

Optional Challenges

1. Write a letter from King Josiah to Jeremiah about the oracles Jeremiah is proclaiming.
2. Suppose Jeremiah had sent his oracle in Jeremiah 2:1—3:5 to the editors of the *Deuteronomic Digest* (a theological quarterly espousing the Deuteronomic viewpoint). Write the editor's reply accepting or rejecting Jeremiah's material.

Memory Verse Suggestions

Before I formed you in the womb I knew you, and before you were born I consecrated you; I appointed you a prophet to the nations. (Jeremiah 1:5; NRSV)

Then the LORD put out his hand and touched my mouth; and the LORD said to me, "Now I have put my words in your mouth. See, today I appoint you over nations and over kingdoms, to pluck up and to pull down, to destroy and to overthrow, to build and to plant." (Jeremiah 1:9–10; NRSV)

Further Reading

Catechism of the Catholic Church, §441, §762, §1611, §2270, §2561, and §2795.
Walter Brueggemann, *An Introduction to the Old Testament: The Canon and Christian Imagination* (Louisville: Westminster John Knox Press, 2003), 177–90.
Abraham Heschel, *The Prophets* (New York: Perennial Classics, 1962), 369–82.
Leslie Hoppe, OFM, *There Shall Be No Poor Among You: Poverty in the Bible* (Nashville: Abingdon Press, 2004), 85–91.

Jeremiah 6:16 "Yahweh says this:
stand at the crossroad and look"

I.8
Jeremiah 7–20

After studying this lesson, you will be able to:

1. Describe the historical, social, and political events during the reign of Jehoiakim of Judah (609–596 BC) that provide the context for the oracles in Jeremiah 7–20.

2. Explain Jeremiah's personal anguish as a prophet in service to the word of God.

3. Recognize the characteristic theological themes of Jeremiah as he proclaims the destruction of Judah.

4. Notice the importance of symbolic actions as a way of communicating the prophetic message.

Read
Jeremiah 7–20; Heschel, pages 146–60; Leclerc, pages 243–51, 255–56, 258–60, 263–65

Geography Task
Using the map on page 22 in your Hammond Atlas, locate the nations that, according to Jeremiah 9:25–26 (9:24–25 NAB and NJB), practiced circumcision.

Important Terms
Confessions/laments of Jeremiah, symbolic prophetic actions, temple sermon, woundedness

Written Work

1. Write a brief sermon based on Jeremiah 7 that a modern prophet might preach outside your parish church on a Sunday morning.

2. Many scholars consider Jeremiah 11:1–12 to be a contribution of Deuteronomic editors. What reminders of themes from the Book of Deuteronomy do you find?

3. What do you learn about Jeremiah from his confessions/laments in:
   a. Jeremiah 11:18—12:6?
   b. Jeremiah 15:10–21?
   c. Jeremiah 17:14–18?
   d. Jeremiah 18:18–23?
   e. Jeremiah 20:7–13?
   f. Jeremiah 20:14–18?

4. Illustrate Jeremiah 17:5–8 in an original art form (picture or drawing, poem, musical composition, etc).

5. What does the parable of the potter (Jer 18:1–12) reveal about:
   a. God and how God relates to the covenant community?
   b. Your own spiritual experience?

Exercise
Using the material in Jeremiah 7–20, add to the time-line of kings and prophets that you began in assignment I.2.

ADDITIONAL SUGGESTIONS FOR THE STUDENT

Optional Challenges

1. Compose a prayer based on Jeremiah 10:23–24 or some other incident in Jeremiah's life.
2. a. List other passages from scripture in which a lesson is drawn from the work of a potter.
   b. What lesson is highlighted in each passage?
3. Read Exodus 32:11–14; Numbers 14:1–19; and 1 Samuel 12:19–25. How do these passages shed light on Jeremiah 15:1? Be specific.

Memory Verse Suggestion

Heal me, O Lord, and I shall be healed; save me, and I shall be saved; for you are my praise. (Jeremiah 17:14; NRSV)

Further Reading

Catechism of the Catholic Church, §150, §2112, and §2584.

Abraham Heschel, *The Prophets* (New York: Perennial Classics, 1962), 202–37.

Joseph Jensen, OSB, *Ethical Dimensions of the Prophets* (Collegeville, MN: Liturgical Press, 2006), 135–43.

Louis Stulman, "Jehoiakim: 1," in Eerdmans *Dictionary of the Bible*, ed. David Noel Freedman (Grand Rapids: William B. Eerdmans Publishing Company, 2000), 679–80.

Jeremiah 17:8 "He is like a tree by the waterside"

I.9
Jeremiah 21–24, 26–33, 36–38, 52

After studying this lesson, you will be able to:

1. Describe the social, political, and historical events (i.e., events that took place during the reign of Zedekiah and led to the Babylonian exile) that formed the background for Jeremiah 21–24, 26–33, 36–38, and 52.

2. Recognize the distinctive emphases of Jeremiah concerning the destruction of Jerusalem and exile as well as glimmers of hope, in particular his prophecy of a new covenant.

Read   Jeremiah 21–24, 26–33, 36–38, 52; Heschel, pages 160–77; Leclerc, pages 242–43, 256–57, 260–63, 265–72 ✓

Geography Task   Using the map on page 23 in your Hammond Atlas, note the extent of the Babylonian Empire.

Important Terms Destruction of Jerusalem, false prophets, new covenant

Written Work
1. a. Briefly summarize, in your own words, the message of Jeremiah to Zedekiah (Jer 21:1–10).
   b. If you were Zedekiah, how would you respond? Be specific.

2. What similarities do you find between the experience of Jeremiah (26:1–12) and that of Jesus? Cite gospel references to support your answer.

3. In Jeremiah 29–33, the prophet offers a message of hope for restoration.
   a. What examples of hope do you find in these chapters?
   b. Which of these examples offer you hope in time of crisis? Why do you find them hopeful?

4. a. What was the message of Jeremiah 31:15–17 for the prophet's community?
   b. How does Matthew 2:16–18 apply Jeremiah 31:15–17 to a different context? Explain.

5. Which aspects of Jeremiah's life can you relate to your own spiritual journey? Explain.

Exercise   Using the material in Jeremiah 21–24, 26–33, 36–38, and 52, add to the time-line of kings and prophets that you began in assignment I.2.

ADDITIONAL SUGGESTIONS FOR THE STUDENT

Optional Challenges

1. Write an original poem or create an original drawing of the destruction of Jerusalem.
2. What passages would you offer to support Jeremiah's view that the LORD wants Babylon to triumph?
3. Why do you think that Jeremiah emphasizes the theme "to pluck up and tear down, to plant and to build"?
4. a. What do we learn about Baruch from the Book of Jeremiah? Cite references.
   b. Do you think that Baruch played a significant role in the mission of Jeremiah? Explain.

Memory Verse Suggestion

The days are surely coming, says the LORD, when I will make a new covenant with the house of Israel and the house of Judah. (Jeremiah 31:31; NRSV)

Further Reading

Catechism of the Catholic Church, §64, §1965, and §2713.

Abraham Heschel, *The Prophets* (New York: Perennial Classics, 1962), 238–48.

Chris A. Rollston, "Jehoiachin," in Eerdmans *Dictionary of the Bible*, ed. David Noel Freedman (Grand Rapids: William B. Eerdmans Publishing Company, 2000), 678–79.

Ronald H. Sack, "Nebuchadnezzar," in Eerdmans *Dictionary of the Bible*, ed. David Noel Freedman (Grand Rapids: William B. Eerdmans Publishing Company, 2000), 953–54.

Louis Stulman, "Zedekiah, 2," in Eerdmans *Dictionary of the Bible*, ed. David Noel Freedman (Grand Rapids: William B. Eerdmans Publishing Company, 2000), 1414.

*Jeremiah 31:15 "Yahweh says this:
a voice is heard in Ramah"*

I.10
Unit One Review

You will be responsible for:

1. A memory verse from one of the prophets that you studied during this unit, indicating the translation used and citing the reference. Pray over it as you review throughout the week.

2. The information included in the following SUPPLEMENTARY READINGS at the back of this workbook:

   #2. "Pre-exilic Prophets: Overview"

   #5. "Self-Quiz: Mid-Unit One"

   #6. "Self-Quiz: Unit One Maps"

3. Demonstrating familiarity with the chronology of major events and people studied during this unit. You do not need to know dates, but must be able to chronologically order major characters and events. (For example, Isaiah of Jerusalem came *before* Jeremiah; Zedekiah came *after* Ahaz.)

UNIT II
Exile and Restoration

After completing this unit, you will be able to:

1. Describe the historical and social situation of Israel during its exile in Babylon.

2. Explain the various theologies that arose from the experiences of exile and return.

3. Recognize the prophetic message of the post-exilic prophets and its implications, especially for the New Testament.

4. Identify the impact of post-exilic theology on the writings of Ezra and Nehemiah.

5. Describe the development of Israel as a community built upon the word during the exile and around the rebuilding of the temple after the return from exile.

Textbooks

Primary Text: The Bible. Use a good translation with scholarly notes.

Other Texts: For helpful background and handy reference we recommend:
Eerdmans *Dictionary of the Bible* (cited as EDB)
Hammond's *Atlas of the Bible Lands* (cited as Hammond Atlas)
Lawrence Boadt's *Reading the Old Testament* (cited as Boadt)
Collegeville *Commentary on Ezekiel, Daniel* (cited as Collegeville Commentary)
Abraham Heschel's *The Prophets* (cited as Heschel)
Thomas L. Leclerc's *Introduction to the Prophets* (cited as Leclerc)

Assignments

Each lesson is to be studied in preparation for your group discussion. For each biblical passage, study the biblical text and footnotes for that particular passage, complete other assigned readings, and do the written work *on a separate page*.

II.1   LAMENTATIONS, OBADIAH

II.2   EZEKIEL 1–5, 8–12, 16–17

II.3   EZEKIEL 18–24, 33–37, 43:1–12, 47:1–12

II.4   ISAIAH 40–48

II.5   ISAIAH 49–55

II.6   HAGGAI, ZECHARIAH 1–8

II.7   ISAIAH 56–66

II.8   EZRA 1:1–11, 3:1—10:17

II.9   NEHEMIAH 1–2, 4–6, 8–10, 13

II.10 UNIT TWO REVIEW

II.1
Lamentations, Obadiah *16 46 11 89*

After studying this lesson, you will be able to:

1. Describe the historical situation surrounding the destruction of Jerusalem and the temple (587/86 BC) and the response of those remaining in the city.

2. Identify the structure, composition, style, and theological themes of the Book of Lamentations and the Book of Obadiah.

3. Explain the literary pattern and theological significance of the lament as a Jewish poetic device.

4. Begin to recognize the central importance of the destruction of Jerusalem and the exile in the experience of the Jewish people.

Read   Lamentations, Obadiah; Leclerc, pages 272–77; EDB articles: "Acrostic" and "Lament"; "The Meaning of Exile," #7 and "Literature of the Exile: Overview—Lamentations and Obadiah," #8 in the SUPPLEMENTARY READINGS at the back of this workbook

Geography Task   Using the map on page 21 in your Hammond Atlas, locate Edom.

Important Terms   Acrostic, lament

Written Work

1. Suppose all the previous books of the Old Testament had been lost in the destruction of Jerusalem and that the only fragment left was Lamentations. What would you know about God? Cite references to support your conclusion.

2. a. What specific persons or groups besides God does the author of Lamentations blame for the terrible disaster that has befallen the people? Cite references.
   b. Do you think the author of Lamentations is correct in his assignment of blame? Why or why not?

3. Which three passages from Lamentations moved you most to a greater sensitivity to the sufferings of the people during the fall of Jerusalem? Why?

4. a. What messages does Lamentations offer for those who suffer disaster? Cite references.
   b. Describe a current situation and explain how the Book of Lamentations might apply to it.

5. a. What is the message of Obadiah in its historical context? Cite references.
   b. What message does the Book of Obadiah have for you?
   c. Why do you think the Book of Obadiah is in the Bible?

1-7, 8-14, 15-21
INDICTMENT   CRIMES   sentencing, Judah's Return

Exercises

1. Using the material in the Book of Lamentations, add to the time-line of kings and prophets that you began in assignment I.2.
2. As you work your way through the unit, choose a verse that you will memorize so that you are able to write it out with the proper citation (translation used and reference [book, chapter, and verse]). Suggestions are given for each lesson, but you may choose another verse that you like.

ADDITIONAL SUGGESTIONS FOR THE STUDENT

Optional Challenges

1. Since Jesus is the new temple, the Liturgy of the Hours for Good Friday applies the lament over the destruction of the temple in Lamentations to his death. If you were selecting passages from Lamentations to use for Good Friday, which ones would you select? Why?
2. Write a lament over the destruction of New Orleans after Hurricane Katrina (or some other devastated city) in the style of Lamentations.

Memory Verse Suggestions

Is it nothing to you, all you who pass by? Look and see if there is any sorrow like my sorrow, which was brought upon me, which the LORD inflicted on the day of his fierce anger. (Lamentations 1:12; NRSV)

For the day of the LORD is near against all the nations. As you have done, it shall be done to you; your deeds shall return on your own head. (Obadiah 15; NRSV)

Further Reading

Catechism of the Catholic Church, §1432.

Lawrence Boadt, *Reading the Old Testament* (New York/Mahwah, NJ: Paulist Press, 1984), 405–12.

Walter Brueggemann, *An Introduction to the Old Testament: The Canon and Christian Imagination* (Louisville: Westminster John Knox Press, 2003), 228–30, 334–43.

Jacopini da Todi, "Stabat Mater," <http://www.campus.udayton.edu/mary/resources/poetry/stbmat.html>.

F. W. Dobbs-Alsopp, *Lamentations*, Interpretation Series: A Bible Commentary for Teaching and Preaching (Louisville: John Knox Press, 2002).

Gregory J. Polan, OSB, "The Book of Lamentations," *The Bible Today* 34, 1 (1996): 15–19.

Lamentations 5:4 "We have to buy our own water to drink"

II.2
Ezekiel 1–5, 8–12, 16–17

After studying this lesson, you will be able to:

1. Describe the social, political, and historical events of the Babylonian exile, in particular as they relate to the person and message of the prophet Ezekiel.

2. Recognize the way Ezekiel expresses his theological message, in particular through the description of his call and his use of imagery, allegories, and symbolic prophetic actions.

3. Identify the structure, composition, and characteristic themes of the Book of Ezekiel.

4. Explain the literary form of allegory and its interpretation.

Read Ezekiel 1–5, 8–12, 16–17; Collegeville Commentary on Ezekiel 1–5, 8–12, 16–17; Leclerc, pages 278–95; "Literature of the Exile: Overview—Ezekiel," #8 in the SUPPLEMENTARY READINGS at the back of this workbook

Geography Task Using the map on page 23 of your Hammond Atlas, locate Nippur. Estimate the number of miles from Jerusalem to Nippur. Note that the exiles would have traveled through the Fertile Crescent and not through the desert. See EDB on the Fertile Crescent.

Important Terms Allegory, Babylonian exile, four living creatures, mortal (son of man), symbolic prophetic action

Written Work

1. a. What do you think are the two most important things to learn about God from Ezekiel's experience in Ezekiel 1? Cite references.
   b. Why do you think that these things are important?

2. a. What significant similarities and differences do you find between the call story of Ezekiel 1:28—3:27 and the call story of either Jeremiah 1:4–19 or Isaiah 6:1–13? Cite references.
   b. How do you think Ezekiel's inability to speak (Ezek 3:26) affected his prophetic ministry? Why?

3. a. Describe the symbolic prophetic actions of Ezekiel in one of the following chapters: Ezekiel 4, 5, or 12. Cite references.
   b. Summarize what you consider to be the meaning of the symbolic actions that you chose. Be specific.

4. a. In the allegory in Ezekiel 17, who or what is
      i. the first eagle?
      ii. the top branch?
      iii. the vine?
      iv. the second eagle?
   b. What do you think is the meaning of the allegory in Ezekiel 17?

5. What event might have the effect on Catholics today that the destruction of Jerusalem had on the people of Judah? Briefly explain your answer.

| **Exercise** | Using the material in Ezekiel 1–5, 8–12, and 16–17, add to the time-line of kings and prophets that you began in assignment I.2. |

ADDITIONAL SUGGESTIONS FOR THE STUDENT

| **Optional Challenges** | 1. Write an original poem or prayer based on Ezekiel's vision of the glory of God leaving the temple. |
| | 2. Write an allegory on a current issue. Share your allegory with your group. See what they understand it to mean. |

| **Memory Verse Suggestion** | I will give them one heart, and put a new spirit within them; I will remove the heart of stone from their flesh and give them a heart of flesh, so that they may follow my statutes and keep my ordinances and obey them. Then they shall be my people, and I will be their God. (Ezekiel 11:19–20; NRSV) |

Further Reading	*Catechism of the Catholic Church*, §219, §715, §1137, and §1296.
	Walter Brueggemann, *An Introduction to the Old Testament: The Canon and Christian Imagination* (Louisville: Westminster John Knox Press, 2003), 191–207.
	Irene Nowell, OSB, "Ezekiel: Difficult Prophet in Difficult Times," *Scripture from Scratch* (July, 2000).

Ezekiel 2:10b

II.3
Ezekiel 18–24, 33–37, 43:1–12, 47:1–12

After studying this lesson, you will be able to:

1. Describe more fully in their historical and social context the person and message of Ezekiel.

2. Recognize specific themes from the Book of Ezekiel, in particular Ezekiel's understanding of God's holiness, individual responsibility, and the hope of restoration for the community after the exile.

Read
Ezekiel 18–24, 33–37, 43:1–12, 47:1–12; Collegeville Commentary on Ezekiel 18–24, 33–37, 43:1–12, 47:1–12; Leclerc, pages 295–303; EDB article: "Shepherd"

Geography Task
Using the map on page 21 of your Hammond Atlas, locate the beginning and end of the symbolic river described in Ezekiel 47:1–12.

Important Terms
Dry bones, individual responsibility, shepherd, spirit

Written Work

1. a. What do Ezekiel 18 and 33:10–20 tell you about individual responsibility? Be specific.
   b. Why do you think that this was an important message for the exiles?
   c. Do you think that this message is important today? Why or why not?

2. a. What events in the history of Israel are described in the allegory found in Ezekiel 23:1–34? Be specific.
   b. In what ways does this allegorical imagery help or hinder your understanding of Israel's past?

3. According to Ezekiel 24:15–27:
   a. Why does God forbid Ezekiel to mourn the death of his wife?
   b. Ezekiel regains his ability to speak. How did his previous silence (see Ezek 3:22–27) contribute to his prophetic role? Be specific.

4. a. Based on your reading of Ezekiel 34:
   i. What happens to sheep without a shepherd?
   ii. What is God's response to sheep without a shepherd?
   b. What parallels do you see between Ezekiel 34 and
   i. Matthew 25:31–46?
   ii. John 10:1–18?

5. a. According to Ezekiel 36–37, 43:1–12, and 47:1–12, what promises are made that would give hope to the exiles? Cite references.
   b. What part of Ezekiel's message of hope is most meaningful for your spiritual journey? Why?

Exercise Using the material in Ezekiel 18–24, 33–37, 43:1–12, and 47:1–12, add to the time-line of kings and prophets that you began in assignment I.2.

ADDITIONAL SUGGESTIONS FOR THE STUDENT

Optional Challenges

1. Compare and contrast the allusions to the exodus generation in Jeremiah 2:2–5 and in Ezekiel 20.
2. Compare and contrast the growing realization of individual responsibility as found in Jeremiah 31:29–30, Lamentations 5:7, and Ezekiel 18 and 33:10–20.
3. Tell the allegory of the two sisters in Ezekiel 23:1–34 as an allegory of two brothers.

Memory Verse Suggestion

Then he said to me, "Mortal [son of man], these bones are the whole house of Israel. They say, 'Our bones are dried up, and our hope is lost; we are cut off completely.' Therefore prophesy, and say to them, Thus says the Lord GOD: I am going to open your graves, and bring you up from your graves, O my people; and I will bring you back to the land of Israel. And you shall know that I am the LORD, when I open your graves, and bring you up from your graves, O my people." (Ezekiel 37:11–13; NRSV)

Further Reading

Catechism of the Catholic Church, §64, §368, §703, §1432, and §2811.
Dorothy Jonaitis, OP, *Unmasking Apocalyptic Texts: A Guide to Preaching and Teaching* (New York/Mahwah, NJ: Paulist Press, 2005), 73–80.

Ezekiel 47:12 "Along the river, on either bank"

II.4
Isaiah 40–48

After studying this lesson, you will be able to:

1. Describe the social, political, and historical events surrounding the end of the exile in Babylon that provide the background for the oracles of Second Isaiah.

2. Recognize the major themes of Second Isaiah, especially the homecoming as a new exodus, images of God as creator, redeemer, and the only God (monotheism).

3. Identify the structure, composition, and literary forms of Second Isaiah.

4. Explain the reasons for distinguishing First Isaiah (Isa 1–39) from Second Isaiah (Isa 40–55).

Read

Isaiah 40–48; Leclerc, pages 304–32; EDB articles: "Cyrus" and "Monotheism, Ancient Israel"; "Literature of the Exile: Overview—Second Isaiah," #8 in the SUPPLEMENTARY READINGS at the back of this workbook

Geography Task

Using the map on page 23 of your Hammond Atlas, locate the Median Empire and the Kingdom of Lydia; and on page 24 of your Hammond Atlas, note the extent of the Persian Empire.

Important Terms

Monotheism, Second Isaiah (Deutero-Isaiah), redeemer

Written Work

1. a. List the passages in Isaiah 40–48 that portray God as creator.
   b. How does Second Isaiah's understanding of God as creator contribute to the emerging concept of monotheism? Be specific.

2. a. How does Second Isaiah describe Cyrus of Persia and his role in God's plan? Cite references.
   b. Do you think that God works in those outside the Christian community to accomplish his will? If not, why not? If so, give one example of a person from the twentieth or twenty-first century and explain your choice.

3. a. Which passages from Isaiah 40–48 suggest that the return of the exiles will be a *new* exodus? Cite references.
   b. Why do you think that Second Isaiah uses exodus imagery?

4. What does Second Isaiah try to teach the Israelites through his mocking treatment of idols (impotent nothings) in Isaiah 40:19–20, 41:6–7 (NAB, found after Isa 40:20), 44:9–20, and 46:6–7?

5. How have New Testament authors used each of the following passages in a different context? Cite references from the New Testament.
   a. Isaiah 40:3–4   c. Isaiah 42:1
   b. Isaiah 40:6–8   d. Isaiah 45:23–24

6. If you were a Jew living in Babylon, which three passages from Isaiah 40–48 would give you the most comfort? Why?

Exercise   Using the material in Isaiah 40–48, add to the time-line of kings and prophets that you began in assignment I.2.

ADDITIONAL SUGGESTIONS FOR THE STUDENT

Optional Challenges
1. Which section from Isaiah 40–48 would be most meaningful to a parish Bible study group during Advent? Develop a plan for leading an Advent Bible study using the text that you have chosen. Be specific.
2. Illustrate some passage from Isaiah 40–48 with an original drawing or poem.
3. How does Second Isaiah continue the language and themes of Isaiah of Jerusalem concerning:
    a. God's holiness? Cite references from First and Second Isaiah.
    b. God's use of foreign rulers? Cite references from First and Second Isaiah.

Memory Verse Suggestions
Comfort, O comfort my people, says your God. Speak tenderly to Jerusalem, and cry to her that she has served her term, that her penalty is paid, that she has received from the LORD's hand double for all her sins. (Isaiah 40:1–2; NRSV)

The grass withers, the flower fades; but the word of our God will stand forever. (Isaiah 40:8; NRSV)

Those who wait for the LORD shall renew their strength, they shall mount up with wings like eagles, they shall run and not be weary, they shall walk and not faint. (Isaiah 40:31; NRSV)

Further Reading
Catechism of the Catholic Church, §201, §206, §218, §219, §711, §754, §2112, and §2167.
Lawrence Boadt, *Reading the Old Testament: An Introduction* (New York/Mahwah, NJ: Paulist Press, 1984), 413–30.
Mark Smith, *Memoirs of God* (Minneapolis: Augsburg Fortress, 2004).
Xenophon, *The Education of Cyrus*, trans. Wayne Ambler (Ithaca, New York: Cornell University Press, 2001).

Isaiah 41:1   "Coasts and isles fall silent before me"

II.5
Isaiah 49–55

After studying this lesson, you will be able to:

1. Describe more fully the characteristic emphases and theology of Second Isaiah as they relate to the historical and social situation of his audience.

2. Recognize important theological themes from Second Isaiah, in particular the Servant of the LORD and the New Jerusalem, as well as to note the use of these themes by early Christian authors.

Read

Isaiah 49–55; Heschel, pages 184–201; EDB article: "Servant of the LORD, Second Isaiah"

Geography Task

Using the map on page 24 of your Hammond Atlas, locate Syene (Sinim).

Important Terms

Servant of the LORD, Servant Songs, suffering

Written Work

1. a. What evidence from the four Servant Songs (Isaiah 42:1–4, 49:1–7, 50:4–9, 52:13–53:12) supports the conclusion that the Servant is:
   i. an individual? Explain. Cite references to support your explanation.
   ii. a personification of Israel? Explain. Cite references to support your explanation.
   b. Using a fuller sense, Christians identify Jesus as the Servant. Find New Testament texts that reflect this fuller sense in *one* of the Servant Songs.
   c. Do you think these views are mutually exclusive? Why or why not?

2. a. What similarity do you see between Second Isaiah's picture of a loving God (Isa 49:14–23) and that of Hosea (11:1–9)?
   b. What is the significance of these two passages for your understanding of God?

Human love is Flawed

3. Second Isaiah sees suffering as redemptive (Isa 53:5, 11, 12).
   a. How can suffering be redemptive?
   b. How have you experienced suffering as redemptive in your life?

4. The church proclaims Isaiah 54:5–14 and Isaiah 55:1–11 at the Easter Vigil. What in these readings do you think makes them appropriate for this celebration? Be specific.

5. To what event in your own life could you compare the return from exile?

Exercise

Using the material in Isaiah 49–55, add to the time-line of kings and prophets that you began in assignment I.2.

ADDITIONAL SUGGESTIONS FOR THE STUDENT

Optional Challenges

1. Imagine you are an exile in Babylon. Write a letter to a relative still in Judah and describe *either*:
   a. your life and the hope you have for returning to Jerusalem *or*
   b. your feelings about wanting to stay in Babylon rather than returning to Jerusalem.
2. a. What references do you find in Isaiah 49–55 to a barren Zion made joyful by her children?
   b. What biblical women experienced this joy? Cite references.
3. What evidence could you cite to support the hypothesis that the Servant might be the prophet Jeremiah? Be specific.

Memory Verse Suggestions

Can a woman forget her nursing child, or show no compassion for the child of her womb? Even these may forget, yet I will not forget you. (Isaiah 49:15; NRSV)

For my thoughts are not your thoughts, nor are your ways my ways, says the LORD. (Isaiah 55:8; NRSV)

Further Reading

Catechism of the Catholic Church, §370, §571, §601, §608, §623, §713, §1502, and §1505.
Richard J. Clifford, SJ, "Prophetic Leader," *The Bible Today* 39, 2 (2001): 69–74.
Chris Franke, "Is There a God and Does God Care?" *The Bible Today* 39, 2 (2001): 83–87.
Claire Mathews McGinnis, "Engaging Israel's Traditions for a New Day," *The Bible Today* 39, 2 (2001): 75–81.
Gregory J. Polan, OSB, "Portraits of Second Isaiah's Servant," *The Bible Today* 39, 2 (2001): 89–93.

Isaiah 49:15 "Can a woman forget the baby at her breast?"

II.6
Haggai, Zechariah 1–8

After studying this lesson, you will be able to:

1. Identify the historical and social context of the return of the exiles and the ways in which they tried to restore their religious beliefs and practice.

2. Describe the person and message of Haggai and First Zechariah and their prophetic contribution to the rebuilding of the Jerusalem temple.

Read

Haggai, Zechariah 1–8; Leclerc, pages 333–46; EDB articles: "Darius, #1," "Satan," and "Zerubbabel"; "Restoration Literature: Overview—Haggai and Zechariah," #9 in the SUPPLEMENTARY READINGS at the back of this workbook

Geography Task

Using the map on page 24 of your Hammond Atlas, note the extent of the post-exilic city of Jerusalem.

Important Terms

Decree (Edict) of Cyrus, restoration, second temple

Written Work

1. a. Why do you think Haggai's vision of restoration stresses the rebuilding of the temple? Be specific.
   b. What need do you see in the church today that is similar to the need for the rebuilding of the temple in Haggai's time? Explain your choice.

2. In your own words, briefly summarize the message of each of Zechariah's first four visions:
   a. Zechariah 1:7–17
   b. Zechariah 1:18–21 (2:1–4 NAB and NJB)
   c. Zechariah 2:1–5 (2:5–9 NAB and NJB)
   d. Zechariah 3:1–10

3. Zechariah was an important source for the Book of Revelation. Using the footnotes and cross-references in your Bible, describe the content of at least three passages in Revelation where Zechariah's images were used as source material.

4. a. What do you learn about the Satan figure in Zechariah 3 from reading Leclerc, pages 344–45?
   b. How does this understanding of Satan relate to the popular notion of Satan today? Be specific.

5. In light of the hopes and prophecies for Zerubbabel in Haggai (2:20–23) and Zechariah (6:11):
   a. What do you think happened to Zerubbabel?
   b. What insight does this give you into post-exilic prophecy?

Exercises

1. Using the material in Haggai and Zechariah 1–8, add to the time-line of kings and prophets that you began in assignment I.2.
2. Review your grasp of the basic information so far by taking the "Self-Quiz: Mid-Unit Two," #10 in the SUPPLEMENTARY READINGS at the back of this workbook.

ADDITIONAL SUGGESTIONS FOR THE STUDENT

Optional Challenges

1. Create an original poem or picture based on some passage of Zechariah.
2. a. What feast occurs on the date given in Haggai 2:1?
   b. How is this feast connected with the rebuilding of the temple?
   c. How is this feast described in Zechariah?

Memory Verse Suggestions

The latter splendor of this house shall be greater than the former, says the LORD of hosts; and in this place I will give prosperity, says the LORD of hosts. (Haggai 2:9; NRSV)

Sing and rejoice, O daughter Zion! For lo, I will come and dwell in your midst, says the LORD. Many nations shall join themselves to the LORD on that day, and shall be my people; and I will dwell in your midst. And you shall know that the LORD of hosts has sent me to you. (Zechariah 2:10–11; NRSV)

Further Reading

Catechism of the Catholic Church, §336, §436, and §2851.
Leslie J. Hoppe, OFM, "Zechariah 3: A Vision of Forgiveness," *The Bible Today* 38, 1 (2000): 10–16.
Alice Laffey, "Zechariah 1: A Vision of Compassion," *The Bible Today* 38, 1 (2000): 5–9.
Beth LaRocca-Pitts, "Zechariah 6: A Vision of Peace," *The Bible Today* 38, 1 (2000): 23–27.
Kathleen S. Nash, "Zechariah 4: A Vision of Small Beginnings," *The Bible Today* 38, 1 (2000): 17–22.

Zechariah 10:11   "Then taking the silver and gold"

After studying this lesson, you will be able to:

1. Describe some of the scholarly reasons for proposing the composite character of the Book of Isaiah and for identifying chapters 56–66 as Third Isaiah.

2. Identify the historical, social, and political events that provide the background for Isaiah 56–66.

3. Recognize the important themes of Third Isaiah, especially universal salvation, purification from sinfulness, and hopes for a new Zion.

4. Explain the possible overall organizational principles in the final editing of the Book of Isaiah.

Read   Isaiah 56–66; Leclerc, pages 360–75; "Restoration Literature: Overview—Third Isaiah," #9 in the SUPPLEMENTARY READINGS at the back of this workbook

Geography Task   Using the footnotes in your Bible and the EDB articles "Ephah (Person), #1," "Kedar," "Midian," "Nebaioth," "Sheba (Place), #2," and "Saba," find the probable location of the places mentioned in Isaiah 60:6–7.

Important Terms   Fasting, holy spirit (Isa 63:10), Third Isaiah (Trito-Isaiah)

Written Work

1. What evidence from Isaiah 56–66 indicates that the temple or surrounding area was in ruins at the time of Third Isaiah? Cite references.

2. Isaiah 56:1–8 and 66:18–23 contain a message of universal salvation. What relevance might this message of universal salvation have for us in our church and civic communities? Be specific.

3. a. Briefly summarize the message about fasting in Isaiah 58:1–12.
   b. How does this passage enrich your understanding of the meaning of fasting during Lent? Be specific.
   c. How might Matthew 25:31–46 have been influenced by Isaiah 58:1–12?

4. Using Isaiah 60:1–6:
   a. What do you think these words meant in their original context?
   b. Why do you think that the church proclaims Isaiah 60:1–6 and Matthew 2:1–12 on Epiphany every year?

5. a. Given the historical situation of Third Isaiah, why do you think that the mission described in Isaiah 61:1–2 was appropriate for the prophet?
   b. In Luke 4:16–21, why would Isaiah 61:1–2 be significant as the text used to describe Jesus' prophetic ministry?

6. What passages in Third Isaiah do you find troubling? Why?

Exercise   Using the material in Isaiah 56–66, add to the time-line of kings and prophets that you began in assignment I.2.

ADDITIONAL SUGGESTIONS FOR THE STUDENT

Optional Challenges
1. Create an original poem or picture depicting Third Isaiah's hopes for Jerusalem.
2. Isaiah 60 has traditionally been used in connection with Christmas and Epiphany. Compose a brief homily on this chapter for one of those feasts.

Memory Verse Suggestion
For I am about to create new heavens and a new earth; the former things shall not be remembered or come to mind. But be glad and rejoice forever in what I am creating; for I am about to create Jerusalem as a joy, and its people as a delight. (Isaiah 65:17–18; NRSV)

Further Reading
Catechism of the Catholic Church, §239, §370, §695, §714, §716, §1286, and §2447.
Lawrence Boadt, *Reading the Old Testament: An Introduction* (New York/Mahwah, NJ: Paulist Press, 1984), 443–47.
Leslie Hoppe, OFM, *There Shall Be No Poor Among You: Poverty in the Bible* (Nashville: Abingdon Press, 2004), 99–102.
Barbara Reid, OP, "What's Biblical about . . . Fasting?" *The Bible Today* 43, 1 (2005): 53–55.

Isaiah 65:25   "The wolf and the young lamb will feed together"

II.8
Ezra 1:1–11, 3:1—10:17

After studying this lesson, you will be able to:

1. Describe the person and mission of Ezra and his role in the spiritual and social restoration of the post-exilic Jewish community.

2. Recognize the important themes of the Book of Ezra, in particular the role of the Jewish law (Torah) in the renewal of Jewish life after the exile.

Read

Ezra 1:1–11, 3:1—10:17; Boadt, pages 453–55; EDB articles: "Beyond the River, #2," "Ezra, #1," "Jews, Judaism," "Persia," "Samaritans," and "Satrap"; "Restoration Literature: Overview—Ezra," #9 in the SUPPLEMENTARY READINGS at the back of this workbook

Geography Task

Using the map on page 24 of your Hammond Atlas, locate the Euphrates River, the eastern boundary of Beyond the River, (West-of-Euphrates [NAB], Transeuphrates [NJB]). Using the map on page 25 of your Hammond Atlas, locate the provinces of Judah and Samaria.

Important Terms

People of the land, Samaritan, satrap
└ Gover␣␣ner

Written Work

1. a. What argument is presented by the Jews in support of the rebuilding of the temple? Cite references.
   b. What arguments are raised by the adversaries of Judah and Benjamin against the rebuilding of the city of Jerusalem, its walls, and the temple? Cite references.
   c. Explain in your own words why the rebuilding of the temple was so important for the returned exiles.

2. a. Do you think that Zerubbabel was right in refusing those who wanted to assist in building the temple in Ezra 4:1–5? Why or why not?
   b. What do you think the message from Ezra 4:1–5 might be for us today? Be specific.

3. Identify three things about Ezra that would lead the post-exilic Jews in Jerusalem to respect him. Explain your choices.

4. Do you think that Ezra was right in denouncing and breaking up marriages with foreigners (Ezra 9:1—10:17)? Why or why not?

5. Maintaining continuity with earlier religious traditions was important to Ezra and his post-exilic community. What three religious traditions do you think that the Catholic Church needs to maintain now and in the future? Why?

Exercise

Using the material in Ezra, add to the time-line of kings and prophets that you began in assignment I.2.

ADDITIONAL SUGGESTIONS FOR THE STUDENT

Optional Challenges

1. Describe Cyrus in an original essay, picture, or poem.
2. Compose a conversation that might have taken place between the people mentioned in Ezra 3:12–13.
3. Imagine that you are the foreign wife of an Israelite man whose marriage was broken up by Ezra. Write a letter to your former spouse describing your thoughts and feelings about the matter.
4. Imagine that you are the Israelite husband of a foreign wife whose marriage was broken up by Ezra. Write a letter to your former spouse describing your thoughts and feelings about the matter.

Memory Verse Suggestion

But now for a brief moment favor has been shown by the LORD our God, who has left us a remnant, and given us a stake in his holy place, in order that he may brighten our eyes and grant us a little sustenance in our slavery. (Ezra 9:8; NRSV)

Further Reading

Catechism of the Catholic Church, §2585.

Walter Brueggemann, *An Introduction to the Old Testament: The Canon and Christian Imagination* (Louisville: Westminster John Knox Press, 2003), 363–74.

Tamara Cohn Eskenazi, "Ezra, Book of," in Eerdmans *Dictionary of the Bible*, ed. David Noel Freedman (Grand Rapids: William B. Eerdmans Publishing Company, 2000), 448–51.

Ezra 3:10   "When the builders had laid the foundation"

Nehemiah 1–2, 4–6 (3:33—6:19 NAB and NJB), 8–10, 13

After studying this lesson, you will be able to:

1. Describe the person and work of Nehemiah in the historical and social context of the restoration of the Jewish community after the exile.

2. Recognize the important themes in the Book of Nehemiah, especially Nehemiah's deep faith in God and his support of Torah and temple as the basis for administrative reforms for the restoration of the Jewish community.

Read

Nehemiah 1–2, 4–6 (3:33—6:19 NAB and NJB), 8–10, 13; Boadt, pages 455–60; EDB article: "Nehemiah, Book of"; "Restoration Literature: Overview—Nehemiah," #9 in the SUPPLEMENTARY READINGS at the back of this workbook

Geography Task

Using the map on page 24 of your Hammond Atlas, note the expansion of the city of Jerusalem under Nehemiah and locate the city of Susa.

Important Terms

Covenant renewal ceremony, restoration

Written Work

1. What evidence from the Book of Nehemiah shows that Nehemiah was a conscientious and capable governor? Cite references.

2. a. What do you learn from the Book of Nehemiah about Nehemiah's prayer life? Be specific.
   b. In what ways could the example of Nehemiah help you in your prayer life? Be specific.

3. a. Identify three problems in the life of the Jewish community that Nehemiah tried to remedy. Cite references.
   b. What parallels do you see between the problems addressed by Nehemiah and problems that we face in the twenty-first century? Be specific.

4. Many scholars believe that Ezra might have been the final redactor of the Torah. What evidence do you find in Nehemiah 8–9 to support that belief?

5. Joshua 24:1–28 and Nehemiah 9–10 describe covenant renewal ceremonies.
   a. What elements in Nehemiah 9–10 were new for the postexilic community?
   b. Why do you think these additions were made? Be specific.

6. Nehemiah was a lay person who worked to build up the community. In their 2005 statement *Co-workers in the Vineyard of the Lord*, the U.S. bishops say, "All of the baptized are called to work toward the transformation of the world." Give several examples of how the Catholic laity might fulfill this call in the contemporary church and in secular society. Be specific.

Exercise   Using the material in Nehemiah, add to the time-line that you began in assignment I.2.

ADDITIONAL SUGGESTIONS FOR THE STUDENT

Optional
Challenges
1. Imagine that you are a servant of Nehemiah. Write a letter to a relative in Susa describing your master's temperament and his activities.
2. Write a paragraph comparing the personalities and work of Ezra and Nehemiah.
3. To help you understand Nehemiah 13:1, summarize three other significant Old Testament passages about the Ammonites and the Moabites.

Memory
Verse
Suggestion
Then Ezra blessed the LORD, the great God, and all the people answered, "Amen, Amen," lifting up their hands. Then they bowed their heads and worshiped the LORD with their faces to the ground. (Nehemiah 8:6; NRSV)

Further
Reading
The Catechism of the Catholic Church, §900, §1669, and §2442.
USCCB, *Co-Workers in the Vineyard of the Lord* (Washington, DC: United States Conference of Catholic Bishops, 2005).

Nehemiah 8:1   "All the people gathered as one"

II.10
Unit Two Review

You will be responsible for:

1. A memory verse from one of the books that you studied during this unit, indicating the translation used and citing the reference. Pray over it as you review throughout the week.

2. The information included in the following SUPPLEMENTARY READINGS at the back of this workbook:

   #8. "Literature of the Exile: Overview"

   #9. "Restoration Literature: Overview"

   #10. "Self-Quiz: Mid-Unit Two"

   #11. "Self-Quiz: Unit Two Map" *Pg 84*

3. Demonstrating familiarity with the chronology of major events and people studied during this unit. You do not need to know dates, but must be able to place in chronological order the major events and characters. (For example, Second Isaiah comes *after* Ezekiel; Lamentations comes *before* Ezra.)

UNIT III
After the Exile

After completing this unit, you will be able to:

1. Describe the historical and social situation of post-exilic Israel.

2. Explain the message of the post-exilic prophets and its implications, especially for the New Testament.

3. Identify how the differing theological perspectives of the Chronicler and the Deuteronomistic Historian impact the writing of historical narratives, in particular by comparing 1 and 2 Chronicles with 1 and 2 Samuel and 1 and 2 Kings.

4. Discuss Hebrew poetry as exemplified in the Song of Solomon (Song of Songs) and the Book of Psalms.

5. Recognize the use of psalms in Christian prayer.

Textbooks

Primary Text: The Bible. Use a good translation with scholarly notes.

Other Texts: For helpful background and handy reference we recommend:
    Eerdmans *Dictionary of the Bible* (cited as EDB)
    Hammond's *Atlas of the Bible Lands* (cited as Hammond Atlas)
    Lawrence Boadt's *Reading the Old Testament* (cited as Boadt)
    Thomas L. Leclerc's *Introduction to the Prophets* (cited as Leclerc)

Assignments

Each lesson is to be studied in preparation for your group discussion. For each biblical passage, study the biblical text and footnotes for that particular passage, complete other assigned readings, and do the written work *on a separate page.*

    III.1 1 CHRONICLES 10–22, 28–29

    III.2 2 CHRONICLES 1–9, 28–36

    III.3 JOEL, MALACHI, ZECHARIAH 9–14

    III.4 RUTH

    III.5 SONG OF SOLOMON (SONG OF SONGS)

    III.6 PSALMS I: HEBREW POETRY AND ITS USE IN CHRISTIAN LITURGY (Psalms 1, 15, 22, 34, 51, 104, 119, 141)

    III.7 PSALMS II: SUPPLICATION AND LAMENT (Psalms 3, 5, 6, 14, 32, 38, 74, 80, 88, 109, 130, 137, 139:19–22)

    III.8 PSALMS III: CONFIDENCE, THANKSGIVING, AND PRAISE (Psalms 2, 8, 23, 27, 29, 30, 33, 45, 48, 62, 65, 72, 91, 92, 100, 101, 110, 113, 116, 118, 124, 131, 132, 148, 150)

    III.9 PSALMS IV: REVIEWING THE STORY OF ISRAEL (Psalms 37, 47, 49, 50, 78, 82, 89, 95, 96, 105, 106, 135, 136)

    III.10 UNIT THREE REVIEW

After studying this lesson, you will be able to:

1. Identify the religious, social, political, and historical situation of the post-exilic Jewish community for which the Books of Chronicles were written.

2. Recognize the Chronicler's reinterpretation of the history of Israel as a covenant relationship that demanded an obedient response to the Mosaic Law.

3. Explain the Chronicler's redaction of his sources, in particular the Deuteronomistic History of Israel.

4. Better understand the expectations of ancient Jewish readers regarding history and the different ways in which history was written.

Read

1 Chronicles 10–22, 28–29; Boadt, pages 449–53; EDB article: "Historiography, Biblical: Biblical Historical Writing"; "David, the King: Two Biblical Portraits," #12, "Synoptic Comparison 1: The Bringing of the Ark to Jerusalem," #13, and "After the Exile: Overview—The Chronicler's History," #14 in the SUPPLEMENTARY READINGS at the back of this workbook

Geography Task

Using the maps on pages 16 and 17 of your Hammond Atlas, locate: Gibeon, Jericho, Hebron, Bethlehem, Jerusalem, Ammon, Gath, Moab, Tyre, and Damascus. How do these places relate to the story of David?

Important Terms

Chronicler, redaction

Written Work

1. Using your Bible and SUPPLEMENTARY READING #13, "Synoptic Comparison 1: The Bringing of the Ark to Jerusalem," answer these questions:
   a. In what ways does the Chronicler edit 2 Samuel 6? Be specific.
   b. How does his editing fit the needs of the post-exilic community: its attitudes, behavior, and roles related to the temple and temple worship?

2. The hymn in 1 Chronicles 16:8–36 is a compilation of a number of psalms.
   a. Which psalms are included?
   b. Why do you think these psalms were selected by the Chronicler?
   c. Why do you think the Chronicler used existing psalms for the hymn rather than composing a new hymn?

3. a. David's military conquests are described in 1 Chronicles 20:1–2 and 2 Samuel 11:1–12:30.
   i. What part of 2 Samuel has the Chronicler omitted? Be specific.
   ii. How does this editing affect the Chronicler's portrait of David?
   iii. How do you feel about the Chronicler's refashioning of the portrait of David? Explain.
   b. In the story of the census of Israel told in 1 Chronicles 21 and 2 Samuel 24:
   i. What has the Chronicler added to 2 Samuel? Be specific.
   ii. How does this editing affect the Chronicler's portrait of David?
   iii. How do you feel about the Chronicler's refashioning of the portrait of David? Explain.

4. a. What differences do you notice between the account of Solomon becoming king in 1 Kings 1–2 and in 1 Chronicles 28–29?
   b. How does the Chronicler's editing affect his portrait of Solomon?
   c. How do you feel about the Chronicler's refashioning of the portrait of Solomon? Explain.

5. In what ways does the Chronicler's portrait of David in 1 Chronicles serve as a model for the post-exilic community? Be specific.

6. Which passage from this week's readings can you relate to your spiritual journey? Why?

Exercises

1. As you work your way through the unit, choose a verse that you will memorize so that you are able to write it out with the proper citation (translation used and reference [book, chapter, and verse]). Suggestions are given for each lesson, but you may choose another verse that you like.
2. Using the material in 1 Chronicles, add to the time-line of kings and prophets that you began in assignment I.2.

ADDITIONAL SUGGESTIONS FOR THE STUDENT

Optional Challenges

1. Create an original drawing of David as the Chronicler portrays him.
2. Write a conversation (perhaps in heaven!) between the Chronicler and the Deuteronomistic Historian about the merits or value of the histories each wrote.

Memory Verse Suggestion

Yours, O LORD, are the greatness, the power, the glory, the victory, and the majesty; for all that is in the heavens and on the earth is yours; yours is the kingdom, O LORD, and you are exalted as head above all. (1 Chronicles 29:11; NRSV)

Further Reading

Catechism of the Catholic Church, §441 and §2585.
Gary N. Knoppers, "Chronicles, Books of" in Eerdmans *Dictionary of the Bible*, ed. David Noel Freedman (Grand Rapids: William B. Eerdmans Publishing Company, 2000), 242–44.

1 Chronicles 28:11   "David then gave his s

III.2
2 Chronicles 1–9, 28–36

After studying this lesson, you will be able to:

1. Describe more fully the situation, message, and theology of the Chronicler's history and its role in post-exilic Judaism.

2. Recognize the major themes of the Chronicler's history, in particular the centrality of the temple for the restored people of Judah.

3. Analyze the way in which the post-exilic Jews used history to further their goals of restoration.

Read 2 Chronicles 1–9, 28–36; EDB article: "Levites"; "After the Exile: Overview—The Chronicler's History," #14, "Synoptic Comparison 2: Solomon's Prayer," #15, and "Prayer of Manasseh," #16 in the SUPPLEMENTARY READINGS at the back of this workbook

Geography Task Using the map on page 18 of your Hammond Atlas, locate Ezion-Geber, Shechem, and Bethel.

Important Terms All Israel, Levites, immediate retribution

Written Work

1. Using SUPPLEMENTARY READING #15, compare 1 Kings 8:54–61 with 2 Chronicles 7:1–4.
   a. Name at least two significant details that the Chronicler has added. Cite references.
   b. In light of the post-exilic situation, why do you think he made these additions?

2. How does 2 Chronicles 7:12–22 summarize the Chronicler's view of the relationship between the Lᴏʀᴅ and the people? Be specific.

⸱kiah are described in 2 Kings 18:1–12. The Chronicler expands these
‥ee chapters (2 Chr 29–31).
⸱e Chronicler has added.
⸱xilic situation, why do you think that he made these additions? Be

⸱s no parallel in 2 Kings 21:1–18.
⸱he Chronicler added these verses about Manasseh? Be specific.
⸱l Prayer of Manasseh in SUPPLEMENTARY READING #16
⸱ssertion that "Manasseh knew that the Lᴏʀᴅ indeed

⸱erpreted history to meet the needs of his community. In
⸱interpreting still done in your personal family history *or*
⸱ırnalism? Give specific examples.
⸱nues to be rewritten and reinterpreted?

Exercise   Using the material in 2 Chronicles, add to the time-line of kings and prophets that you began in assignment I.2.

ADDITIONAL SUGGESTIONS FOR THE STUDENT

Optional Challenges

1. Draw an original diagram of Solomon's temple or of some part of it.
2. a. Describe the character of Solomon as the Chronicler portrays him.
   b. How would Solomon be a model for the Chronicler's community?
3. Write an original prayer modeled on King Solomon's prayer at the dedication of the temple that would be appropriate for the dedication of a new parish church today.
4. What sources does the Chronicler say he is using? Cite references.

Memory Verse Suggestion

O LORD, God of Israel, there is no God like you, in heaven or on earth, keeping covenant in steadfast love with your servants who walk before you with all their heart. (2 Chronicles 6:14; NRSV)

Further Reading

Catechism of the Catholic Church, §756.
Walter Brueggemann, *An Introduction to the Old Testament: The Canon and Christian Imagination* (Louisville: Westminster John Knox Press, 2003), 375–82.

2 Chronicles 22:11   "Rescued Joash—put him with his nurse—"

III.3
Joel, Malachi, Zechariah 9–14 —

Poetry difficult
He is not mentioned
No Visions
No Zerubbabel
No temple emph.

After studying this lesson, you will be able to:

1. Identify the social, political, and historical situations that provoked the prophetic oracles of Joel, Malachi, and Deutero-Zechariah.

2. Recognize the structure, message, prophetic styles, and theological themes that characterize the prophecies of Joel, Malachi, and Deutero-Zechariah.

3. Note how the New Testament writers used passages from Joel, Malachi, and Deutero-Zechariah to clarify their understanding of New Testament events.

Read

Joel, Malachi, Zechariah 9–14; Leclerc, pages 346–59 and 375–82; EDB article: "Locust"; "After the Exile: Overview—Joel, Malachi, and Deutero-Zechariah," #14 in the SUPPLEMENTARY READINGS at the back of this workbook

Geography Task

What geographical locations are indicated in Joel 2:20 by the "parched and desolate land," the "eastern sea," and the "western sea"? Using the map on page 7 of your Hammond Atlas, locate Megiddo and the Plain of Esdralon.

Important Terms

Apocalyptic vision, teaching dialogue

Written Work

1. Why do you think Luke selects Joel 2:28–32 (3:1–5 NAB and NJB) as the text for the first Christian sermon delivered by Peter at Pentecost (Acts 2:1–21)?

2. What might have caused Joel (3:10 [4:10 NAB and NJB]) to reverse the advice given in Isaiah 2:4 and Micah 4:3?

3. a. Of what sin are the people accused in Malachi 2:10–16?
   b. What do you learn about Malachi's understanding of marriage from this passage?
   c. Do you think that Malachi's message on marriage is relevant in the twenty-first century? Why or why not?

4. Matthew seems to have been familiar with Malachi's prophecy (Mal 3:1—4:6, [3:1–24 NAB and NJB]).
   a. How does Matthew use Malachi to help gospel readers understand John the Baptist in
      i. Matthew 3:1–12?
      ii. Matthew 11:2–14?
      iii. Matthew 17:9–13?
   b. How does Matthew's connection of John the Baptist with Elijah help Matthew's community to understand who Jesus is?

5. Formulate a brief "teaching dialogue" in the style of Malachi that you could use to help someone understand *one* of the following biblical themes: God's love, reconciliation, or social justice.

6. a. Using Zechariah 9:9–10:
      i. What do you think these verses meant to the original audience?
      ii. How does Matthew 21:1–11 interpret these verses?
   b. Using Zechariah 12:10:
      i. What do you think this verse meant to the original audience?
      ii. How does John 19:37 interpret this text?

Exercise   Using the material in Joel, Malachi, and Deutero-Zechariah, add to the time-line of kings and prophets that you began in assignment I.2.

ADDITIONAL SUGGESTIONS FOR THE STUDENT

Optional Challenges
1. Present Joel's locust plague in an original poem or picture.
2. Compose an original prayer or draw a picture based on Malachi 1:11.
3. In John 1:19–28, John the Baptist claims explicitly that he is not Elijah. How might you reconcile this with the Matthean tradition (Matt 3:1–12, 11:2–14, 17:9–13) in which John is referred to as Elijah?

Memory Verse Suggestions

Then afterward I will pour out my spirit on all flesh; your sons and your daughters shall prophesy, your old men shall dream dreams, and your young men shall see visions. (Joel 2:28; NRSV)

See, I am sending my messenger to prepare the way before me, and the Lord whom you seek will suddenly come to his temple. The messenger of the covenant in whom you delight—indeed, he is coming, says the LORD of hosts. (Malachi 3:1; NRSV)

Rejoice greatly, O daughter Zion! Shout aloud, O daughter Jerusalem! Lo, your king comes to you; triumphant and victorious is he, humble and riding on a donkey, on a colt, the foal of a donkey. (Zechariah 9:9; NRSV)

Further Reading

Catechism of the Catholic Church, §559, §678, §715, §1287, §1611, and §2561.

Lawrence Boadt, *Reading the Old Testament* (New York/Mahwah, NJ: Paulist Press, 1984), 462–66.

Dorothy Jonaitis, OP, *Unmasking Apocalyptic Texts: A Guide to Preaching and Teaching* (New York/Mahwah, NJ: Paulist Press, 2005), 82–90.

Malachi 3:20
"But for you who fear my name the sun of justice will rise"

III.4
Ruth

After studying this lesson, you will be able to:

1. Describe the literary form of the Book of Ruth as a short story about an ancestor of David.

2. Recognize how the author employs plot, character, setting, and themes.

3. Identify specific themes of the Book of Ruth, especially divine providence, covenant fidelity, and openness to foreigners.

Read

Ruth; Boadt, pages 500–01; EDB articles: "Gleaning," "Levirate Marriage," and "Ruth, Book of"; "After the Exile: Overview—Ruth," #14 in the SUPPLEMENTARY READINGS at the back of this workbook ✔

Geography Task

Using the map on page 21 of your Hammond Atlas, locate Edom and trace the probable route for the journey of Naomi and Ruth from Moab back to Bethlehem. Estimate the distance that they had to travel.

Important Terms

Gleaning, Levirate marriage

Written Work

1. a. Two laws that are important in the story of Ruth are Levirate marriage and leaving grain for the poor to glean. Cite references from the Pentateuch that refer to these laws.
   b. What do you think the purpose of each of these laws was?

2. a. What role does God play in the Book of Ruth? Cite references to support your answer.
   b. Why do you think the author deals with God in this way?

3. Using references from the Book of Ruth, write a brief *character* sketch of *one* of the following: Naomi, Ruth, or Boaz. Remember that a character sketch does not simply describe what a person does, but rather it is a description of the person's personality and attitudes.

4. Some scholars have suggested that the Book of Ruth can best be understood as a type of dissent literature (like Isa 56:1–7) in reaction to the narrow exclusivism of some other writers in the post-exilic community. What evidence do you find in this book that might support that interpretation? Cite references.

5. Describe an event in the life of your family or the family of someone you know that was like some event in the Book of Ruth.

ADDITIONAL SUGGESTIONS FOR THE STUDENT

Optional Challenges

1. Imagine that you are Naomi and that your grandson, Obed, asks you to tell him the story of your life. What would you say?
2. Describe at least two other significant incidents involving Moab in the Old Testament.
3. Create an original poem or drawing based on the Book of Ruth.

Memory Verse Suggestion

But Ruth said, "Do not press me to leave you or to turn back from following you! Where you go, I will go; where you lodge, I will lodge; your people shall be my people, and your God my God." (Ruth 1:16; NRSV)

Further Reading

Catechism of the Catholic Church, §1829, §1939, §1944, and §1948.
Macrina Scott, OSF, *Bible Stories Revisited: Discover Your Story in the Old Testament* (Cincinnati: St. Anthony Messenger Press, 1999), 131–42.
Phyllis Trible, *God and the Rhetoric of Sexuality* (Philadelphia: Fortress Press, 1978), 166–99.

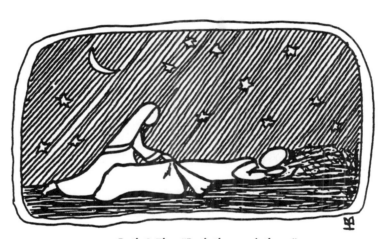

Ruth 3:7b   "Ruth then quietly..."

III.5
Song of Solomon (Song of Songs)

After studying this lesson, you will be able to:

1. Identify the Song of Solomon (Song of Songs) as Hebrew poetry by examining its structure, images, and symbols.

2. Recognize the connection between human and divine love as illustrated through the collection of love lyrics in the Song of Solomon (Song of Songs).

3. Explain possible allegorical interpretations of the Song of Solomon (Song of Songs).

Read   Song of Solomon (Song of Songs); Boadt, pages 485–86; EDB articles: "Allegory," "Poetry," and "Song of Solomon"; "After the Exile: Overview—Song of Solomon (Song of Songs)," #14 in the SUPPLEMENTARY READINGS at the back of this workbook

Geography Task   Using the map on page 21 of your Hammond Atlas, locate Engedi (Song 1:14); Sharon (Song 2:1); Gilead (Song 4:1, 6:5); Lebanon, Hermon (Song 4:8); Tirzah (Song 6:4); Heshbon (Song 7:5); and Mt. Carmel (Song 7:6). Notice how the Song of Solomon (Song of Songs) describes the beauty of places throughout the Holy Land.

Important Term   Allegory

Written Work

1. Describe at least two other places in the Bible where the love of God for his people is compared to the love between a man and a woman. Cite references.

2. Choose one passage from the Song of Solomon (Song of Songs). Show how this passage might be interpreted by
   a. a person who considers the Song of Solomon (Song of Songs) an allegory about the relationship between God and his people Israel or Christ and the church.
   b. a person who considers the Song of Solomon (Song of Songs) an allegory about the relationship between God and the individual human person.
   c. a person who considers the Song of Solomon (Song of Songs) poetry about human love.

3. Choose an image or metaphor used in Song of Solomon (Song of Songs) 1–4.
   a. What do you think the author was trying to convey by using this image or metaphor?
   b. What meaning does this image or metaphor have for you?

4. Choose one of the descriptions of the beloved (e.g., Song 4:1–11, 5:9–16, 6:4–10) and rewrite it using modern imagery.

5. In the New American Bible preface to Song of Songs, we read that "the poem is not an allegory in which each remark, e.g., in the dialogue of the lovers, has a higher meaning. It is a parable in which the true meaning of mutual love comes from the poem as a whole." Read in this way, how do you think the poem as a whole sheds new light on the true meaning of mutual love?

Exercise Review your grasp of the basic information covered so far by taking the "Self-Quiz: Mid-Unit Three," #17 in the SUPPLEMENTARY READINGS at the back of this workbook.

ADDITIONAL SUGGESTIONS FOR THE STUDENT

Optional Challenges
1. Do research on six of the plants and/or animals mentioned in the Song of Solomon (Song of Songs). Summarize the most interesting information you found on each.
2. How would you use material from the Song of Solomon (Song of Songs) to explain to a class of adults the way God loves us? Be specific.

Memory Verse Suggestion
Set me as a seal upon your heart, as a seal upon your arm; for love is strong as death, passion fierce as the grave. Its flashes are flashes of fire, a raging flame. Many waters cannot quench love, neither can floods drown it. If one offered for love all the wealth of his house, it would be utterly scorned. (Song of Solomon [Song of Songs] 8:6–7; NRSV)

Further Reading
Catechism of the Catholic Church, §1611 and §2709.
John J. Pilch, "A Window on the Biblical World: Solomon's, the Best of All Songs," *The Bible Today* 44, 6 (2006): 385–89.

Song of Songs 2:3
"As an apple tree—in his delightful shade sit and his fruit is sweet"

III.6
Psalms I: Hebrew Poetry and Its Use in Christian Liturgy

After studying this lesson, you will be able to:

1. Describe the diversity of genres in the Book of Psalms.

2. Explain some of the structural features of Hebrew poetry, in particular the use of parallelism and alphabetic construction.

3. Recognize how the images and themes of the psalms were used by Christians to illuminate their understanding of God and Jesus.

4. Explain the use of the psalms in Christian prayer.

Read Psalms 1, 15, 22, 34, 51, 104, 119, 141; Boadt, pages 279–90; "After the Exile: Overview—Psalms," #14 in the SUPPLEMENTARY READINGS at the back of this workbook

Geography Task Using the map on page 21 of your Hammond Atlas, locate Bashan. Using the map on page 48 of your Hammond Atlas, locate the cedars of Lebanon.

Important Term Parallelism: antithetic and synonymous

Written Work

1. Identify the type of parallelism found in each of these psalm verses. Use *S* to indicate synonymous, *A* to indicate antithetic, and *O* to indicate some other pattern.

   a. i. Psalm 1:6
      ii. Psalm 15:1
      iii. Psalm 22:12 (22:13 NAB)
      iv. Psalm 34:10 (34:11 NAB)
      v. Psalm 34:13 (34:14 NAB)
      vi. Psalm 34:19 (34:20 NAB)
      vii. Psalm 51:7 (51:9 NAB)
      viii. Psalm 51:13 (51:15 NAB)
      ix. Psalm 104:28
      x. Psalm 119:72
      xi. Psalm 119:105
      xii. Psalm 141:3

   b. Identify the verse that you think uses parallelism most effectively and briefly explain the reason for your choice.

2. a. Psalm 104 and Genesis 1 share a similar view of the created world. Identify three points of similarity.
   b. How does the psalm enhance your experience of God as creator?

3. Choose *one* of the following psalms: 1, 15, 34, 51, or 141.
   a. How do you feel about it? Be specific.
   b. When would you use this psalm in prayer?
   c. How would you apply it to your own life?
   d. Are there aspects of the psalm that you find surprising, puzzling, or offensive? Explain.

handwritten: 15-34 Recite

CAST
Mark 15:24 — LOTS
matt 27:46 recite

John 19:29 Lots

4. Many Christian authors relate Psalm 22 to the passion and death of Jesus.
   a. Do you think this comparison is justified? Why or why not?
   b. Indicate how one of the evangelists uses this psalm. Cite references.

5. Psalm 119 praises the law (Torah).
   a. Identify some of the synonyms for the law that the author uses. Cite references.
   b. Briefly summarize the psalmist's understanding of the law.

6. Choose psalm texts from this lesson that would be appropriate for greeting cards for *one* of these occasions: a birthday, an anniversary, an illness, the birth of a child, etc. Indicate the occasion and explain why you chose each particular text.

ADDITIONAL SUGGESTIONS FOR THE STUDENT

Optional Challenges

1. Compose a psalm for our own times, using the style of Hebrew poetry as a model.
2. Ancient Israel did not invent the style of poetry used in the psalms. It is common in many ancient Near Eastern cultures. Compare Psalm 104 with the Egyptian Hymn to Aton. Indicate two similarities and two differences.
3. Create an original illustration of a psalm passage.

Memory Verse Suggestions

The LORD is near to the brokenhearted,
and saves the crushed in spirit. (Psalm 34:18; NRSV)

You desire truth in the inward being;
therefore teach me wisdom in my secret heart. (Psalm 51:6; NRSV)

Let my prayer be counted as incense before you,
and the lifting up of my hands as an evening sacrifice. (Psalm 141:2; NRSV)

Further Reading

Catechism of the Catholic Church, §1156, §1177, and §2585–§2597.
Nancy Marie de Flon, *The Joy of Praying the Psalms* (New Jersey: Resurrection Press, 2005).
Roland E. Murphy, O Carm, *The Gift of the Psalms* (Peabody, MA: Hendrickson Publishers, 2000).
Irene Nowell, OSB, "David: Patron Saint of the Psalms," *The Bible Today* 42, 3 (2004): 149–53.
V. Steven Parrish, *A Story of the Psalms: Conversation, Canon, and Congregation* (Collegeville, MN: Liturgical Press, 2003).
Michael Patella, OSB, "Seer's Corner: Psalmody and Psalters," *The Bible Today* 39, 3 (2001): 164–69.

Psalm 15:1   "Yahweh, who can find a home in your tent?"

III.7
Psalms II: Supplication and Lament

After studying this lesson, you will be able to:

1. Describe the structure and characteristic themes of the lament form as used in Hebrew poetry.
2. Recognize the lament psalms and reflect on their function in the liturgical and social life of ancient Israel.
3. Recognize the application and use of the lament psalms for your own prayer.
4. Identify the distinctive literary forms of the psalms.

Read

Fools

Psalms 3, 5, 6, 88 (individual laments); Psalms 14, 74, 80, 137 (communal laments); Psalms 32, 38, 130 (penitential psalms); Psalms 109, 139:19–22 (cursing psalms); EDB articles: "Curse," "Lament," and "Sheol", "Types of Psalms," #18 in the SUPPLEMENTARY READINGS at the back of the student workbook

Geography Task

Using the map on page 23 of your Hammond Atlas, locate the rivers of Babylon.

Important Terms

Cursing psalms, lament psalms, penitential psalms, Sheol

Written Work

1. a. Choose two individual lament psalms. For each, describe the reasons why God's help is being requested.
   b. Choose two communal lament psalms. For each, describe the reasons why God's help is being requested.

2. Do you think the author of Psalm 6 believed in a meaningful afterlife (heaven)? Why or why not? Cite references to support your position.

3. a. Choose a current news story and briefly describe it.
   b. Compose an original individual or communal lament in response to the story. (Remember to follow the lament form and to use synonymous and antithetic parallelism.)

4. Jeremiah's confessions (Jeremiah 11:18—12:6, 15:10–21, 17:14–18, 18:18–23, 20:7–13, 20:14–18) have sometimes been referred to as individual laments. Choose *one* of these confessions and compare it to *one* of the individual lament psalms from this assignment.

5. A number of the psalms include curses against the psalmist's enemies (e.g., Pss 109 and 139). Do you think this type of psalm is ever appropriate for our use as Christians? Why or why not?

ADDITIONAL SUGGESTIONS FOR THE STUDENT

**Optional
Challenge**

Creatively express one of the psalms through an original illustration or musical setting.

**Memory
Verse
Suggestions**

Out of the depths I cry to you, O LORD.
Lord, hear my voice! (Psalm 130:1–2a; NRSV)

By the rivers of Babylon—
there we sat down and there we wept
when we remembered Zion. (Psalm 137:1; NRSV)

**Further
Reading**

Catechism of the Catholic Church, §1850, §2100, and §2629–§2633.
Anthony R. Ceresko, OSFS, "Prayers for Times of Distress," *The Bible Today* 41, 4 (2003): 223–28.
Leslie J. Hoppe, OFM, *There Shall Be No Poor Among You: Poverty in the Bible* (Nashville: Abingdon Press, 2004), 122–30.
Anne Marie Sweet, "Pilgrimage and Reconciliation," *The Bible Today* 38, 3 (2000): 151–55.

Psalm 3:5   "—as for me, if I lie down and sleep"

III.8
Psalms III: Confidence, Thanksgiving, and Praise

After studying this lesson, you will be able to:

1. Identify the structure, characteristic themes, and situations that give rise to the psalms of confidence, thanksgiving, and praise.

2. Recognize the royal psalms and reflect on their function in the liturgical and social life of ancient Israel.

3. Appreciate the theological diversity and the emotional variety expressed in the psalms.

4. Consider how the psalms of confidence, thanksgiving, and praise might be used in your own prayer.

Read

Psalm 23 and *one* of the following: 27, 62, 91, 131 (psalms of confidence/trust); *one* of the following: 30, 92, 116 (psalms of individual thanksgiving); Psalm 118 and *one* of the following: 65, 124 (psalms of communal thanksgiving); Psalms 8, 29, 33, 48, 100 and *one* of the following: 113, 148, 150 (psalms of praise) Psalm 110 and *one* of the following: 2, 45, 72, 101, 132 (royal psalms)

Geography Task

As a geography review, locate the following places on the map on page 21 in your Hammond Atlas: Damascus, Tyre, Gilead, Ammon, Dan, Beersheba, Jericho, Hebron, Bethlehem, Samaria (the city), Jerusalem, Syria, Phoenicia, Philistia, Moab, Edom, the Sea of Galilee, the Dead Sea, and the Mediterranean Sea.

Important Terms

Confidence/trust psalms, praise psalms, thanksgiving psalms

Written Work

1. In Psalms 8, 29, 33, 48, and 100, for what are we invited to praise God? Work with each psalm separately. Cite references.

2. a. What do you think Psalm 110 meant in its original historical setting?
   b. Describe one of the ways in which the early Christians applied this psalm to Jesus. Cite a reference.

3. What words and phrases in Psalm 118 support the conclusion that this psalm was originally used as a part of a thanksgiving celebration in the temple?

4. a. Choose *one* individual thanksgiving psalm. Describe the reasons for which the psalmist gives thanks.
   b. Choose *one* communal thanksgiving psalm (*not* Ps 118). Describe the reasons for which the psalmist gives thanks.

5. In the psalms of confidence/trust, what specific characteristics of God are important for establishing the basis of our trust? Cite references.

6. Write your own psalm of confidence, thanksgiving, or praise. (Remember to follow the general pattern of the hymn: invitation, reasons, and conclusion. Include synonymous and antithetic parallelism.)

ADDITIONAL SUGGESTIONS FOR THE STUDENT

Optional Challenge

Create an original illustration of one of the psalms in this lesson.

Memory Verse Suggestions

O Lord, my heart is not lifted up,
my eyes are not raised too high;
I do not occupy myself with things
too great and too marvelous for me. (Psalm 131:1; NRSV)

It is good to give thanks to the Lord,
to sing praises to your name, O Most High;
to declare your steadfast love in the morning,
and your faithfulness by night. (Psalm 92:1–2; NRSV)

Let everything that breathes praise the Lord! (Psalm 150:6; NRSV)

Further Reading

Catechism of the Catholic Church, §239, §447, §1808, and §2639–§2649.
Michael L. Barré, SS, "Psalm 110: A Journey in Faith and Understanding," *The Bible Today* 44, 6 (2006): 348–52.
Joan Cook, SC, "The Psalms of Thanksgiving," *The Bible Today* 41, 4 (2003): 229–35.
John C. Endres, SJ, "Hymns of Praise," *The Bible Today* 41, 4 (2003): 217–22.
Craig Morrison, OCarm, "A Covenant Forever," *The Bible Today* 44, 6 (2006): 353–58.
Gregory J. Polan, OSB, "The Reign of God and His Anointed One," *The Bible Today* 44, 6 (2006): 337–42.
Roberta L. Salvador, MM, "Psalm 72: The Royal King," *The Bible Today* 44, 6 (2006): 343–47.

Psalm 23:1–2   "Yahweh is my shepherd, I lack nothing"

III.9
Psalms IV: Reviewing the Story of Israel

After studying this lesson, you will be able to:

1. Recognize the use of psalms to recount and illuminate the major events of Israelite history.

2. Note how the psalms express a theology of God in relation to the world and the people of Israel.

3. Appreciate how the psalms express the feelings and moods that we have in our relationship with God.

Read

Psalms 78, 105, 106, 135, 136 (narratives/historical psalms) Psalms 50, 82 (prophetic psalms) Psalms 37, 49 (wisdom psalms) Psalms 47, 95, 96 (The LORD is King) Psalm 89 (messianic psalm); "Rereadings (Relectures)," #19 in the SUPPLEMENTARY READINGS at the back of this workbook

Geography Task

Using the map on page 21 of your Hammond Atlas, review the locations of the following places mentioned in the narrative psalms: Bashan, Canaan, Egypt, Red Sea, and Shiloh.

Important Terms

Messianic psalms, narrative/historical psalms, prophetic psalms, rereading, wisdom psalms

Written Work

1. THEME: MOSAIC COVENANT. Using Psalms 135 and 136:
   What do you consider the three most important things that these psalms remind us of in our covenant relationship with God? Why?

2. THEME: DAVIDIC COVENANT. Using Psalm 89:1–37 (89:1–38 NAB):
   a. What promises does God make to David and his descendants? Cite references.
   b. What role do David and his descendants have in the fulfillment of the promise?
   c. What evidence do you find to support the idea that Psalm 89:38–48 (89:39–49 NAB) was added to the psalm as a result of the exile?

3. THEME: RETRIBUTION and JUDGMENT. Using Psalm 37:
   a. Summarize the psalmist's view of God's way of rewarding the good and punishing the wicked.
   b. Do you think our Christian view today is different from the view of the psalmist? Why or why not?

4. THEME: GOD ALONE IS SUPREME. Using Psalms 47, 95, 96:
   a. For what reason is God identified as king in each psalm?
   b. According to each psalm, what is the appropriate human response to God's sovereignty?
   c. In what practical ways can you respond to the reign of God in your life? Be specific.

5. THEME: CONVERSION. Using Psalms 50 and 82:
   a. How would you summarize the challenge to behavior that these psalms present?
   b. Choose one of the prophets studied this year. Compare the message of that prophet to the message found in Psalms 50 and 82.

Exercise   Review or add the following important dates in Israelite history to the time-line that you began in assignment 1.2: ca.1250 BC, 1000 BC, 922 BC, 722/21 BC, 587/86 BC, 538 BC, 515 BC.

ADDITIONAL SUGGESTIONS FOR THE STUDENT

Optional Challenges

1. Compose an original narrative psalm that includes the high points of Israelite history.
2. Compare and contrast the presentation of Israelite history in Psalms 105 and 106.
    a. Which events are mentioned and which are left out?
    b. What might be the reason for the differences?
3. Note evidence of polytheistic attitudes in the following psalms (Ps 82:1, 5; Ps 89:6–8 [89:7–8 NAB]; Ps 95:3).
    a. What does the evidence tell you about the rise of monotheism in Israel?
    b. What does it tell you about the antiquity of these portions of the psalms?

Memory Verse Suggestions

Take delight in the LORD, and he will give you the desires of your heart.
Commit your way to the LORD; trust in him, and he will act. (Psalm 37:4–5; NRSV)

Clap your hands, all you peoples;
shout to God with loud songs of joy. (Psalm 47:1; NRSV)

Further Reading

Catechism of the Catholic Church, §30, §269, §2628, and §2659.
Dianne Bergant, CSA, "Psalms of Historical Recital," *The Bible Today* 41, 4 (2003): 209–15.
Irene Nowell, OSB, "War and Peace in the Psalms: How to Pray in Times of Crisis," *The Bible Today* 46, 3 (2008): 149–53.
Michael Patella, OSB, "Seers' Corner: Lands of the Psalms," *The Bible Today* 41, 4 (2003): 237–41.

Psalm 136:7–9   "He made the great lights..."

III.10
Unit Three Review

You will be responsible for:

1. A memory verse from one of the books that you studied during this unit, indicating the translation used and citing the reference. Pray over it as you review throughout the week.

2. The information included in the following SUPPLEMENTARY READINGS at the back of this workbook:

   #14. "After the Exile: Overview"

   #17. "Self-Quiz: Mid-Unit Three"

   #20. "Self-Quiz: Unit Three Maps"

3. Identifying the historical order of major events in biblical history using the time-line of kings and prophets that you began in assignment I.2.

Express your appreciation for the members of your study group

The aim of this exercise is to express your appreciation for the members of your small group this year.

1. Take the name of one person in your small group.

2. Make sure that each person in the group has selected a name; contact absent members.

3. Write a brief testimonial about the gift that person's presence has been to your group during this year. Perhaps a guideline could be this message from Paul to the Ephesians (4:25–32 in part):

   So then, putting away falsehood, let all of us speak the truth to our neighbors, for we are members of one another...Let no evil talk come out of your mouths, but only what is useful for building up, as there is need, so that your words may give grace to those who hear...and be kind to one another, tenderhearted, forgiving one another, as God in Christ has forgiven you.

4. Bring your testimonial and share it with the group next week. After sharing with the group, present it to the person about whom you wrote.

Since you will be in a different group next year, you should reflect on the fact that new insights about your faith journey this year have come not only from your personal study but also from working together in your group week after week. Take to heart the words of the U.S. bishops' letter on evangelization, *Go and Make Disciples* (1992):

Conversion is the change of our lives which comes about through the power of the Holy Spirit. All who accept the Gospel undergo a change as we continually put on the mind of Christ by rejecting sin and becoming more faithful disciples in the church. Unless we undergo conversion, we have not truly accepted the Gospel.

Supplementary Readings

1. Classical Prophets: Differentia from Early Prophets

Joseph Jensen, OSB

One objective difference between the earlier prophets and the so-called classical prophets . . . is the existence of books composed of collections of oracles bearing the names of the latter. That alone can still leave the terminology somewhat arbitrary, but there are also discernible differences between the canonical/classical prophets and their predecessors that may be listed as three in number: (1) the sense of call or vocation, (2) a mission that is totally identified with being a bearer of God's word, and (3) the depth of the content of teaching.

Sense of Vocation

Nothing is told of the call of early prophets except in the cases of Samuel and Elisha. In the case of Samuel we are no doubt dealing with a later literary composition intended to enhance Samuel's prophetic standing rather than a personal account of how he became a prophet, and in the case of Elisha there is simply an external action, namely, Elijah throwing his cloak over him—which relates more to his becoming the successor of Elijah than to a call from God as such.

Several of the classical prophets, on the other hand, give us circumstantial, first-person accounts of their call; that alone tells us it must have been important to them. The call narrative is intended as a legitimation of the prophet and his message. This was especially important if, as was often the case, the content of his message was unpopular or subject to challenge. So when Amos was ordered by Amaziah to be off to his native Judah and

cease stirring up trouble at the Bethel sanctuary, Amos replied that he was/is no prophet,[1] but that the Lord took (*lāqah*) him from his previous work and said, "Go, prophesy to my people Israel," which empowers him to say, "Now hear the word of the Lord" (Amos 7:15–16). Jeremiah, who is told he had been chosen to be a prophet before his birth, does not gladly receive the call and alleges his youth as a reason why he should not be sent, to which objection the Lord responds: "To whomever I send you, you shall go; / whatever I command you, you shall speak," and the Lord himself places his words in his mouth (Jer 1:7). Later there is a time when he is on the point of being put to death for giving out threats against Jerusalem and the Temple, and his defense is "I am in your hands; do with me what you think good and right. But mark well: if you put me to death, it is innocent blood you bring upon yourselves . . . For in truth it was the Lord who sent me to you, to speak all these things for you to hear" (26:14–15). The need for such defense is clear from the account of his ministry and career: his message was unpopular and appeared to many to be both seditious and irreverent; because of it he was imprisoned, put in the stocks, left to die in an old cistern. Isaiah's account of his call (Isaiah 6) is undoubtedly formulated, in part at least, to vindicate a message that put him at odds with the rulers and the most influential people of the time; he was probably accused of conspiracy. Ezekiel's call is spread over three chapters (Ezekiel 1–3), and though conflict is not so dramatically clear in his career, he is warned of the resistance he will meet (2:3–8; 3:5–11), and the word of the Lord comes to him even more concretely than it did to Jeremiah, in the form of a scroll he is to eat (2:8—3:4). Even the story of Jonah, fictional though it is, provides a good insight into Israel's understanding of the inescapable nature of the Lord's call. Jonah, commanded by the Lord to go to Nineveh, boards a seagoing ship headed as far as possible in the other direction. But the Lord prepares a storm and then a fish to take Jonah back to his starting point. When "the word of the Lord came to Jonah a second time" (3:1), Jonah's obedience to it could no longer be in doubt.

It is hardly possible for us to explain exactly what lies behind these call narratives. Almost certainly there is a religious experience of some sort that, with no intention of denigrating ecstaticism, I would suggest is something quite different from that of the ecstatic prophets. It is partly on this basis that Albright distinguishes between "the age of the great natural prophets, which came to an end in the ninth century, and that of the literary prophets, which began several decades later," for, as he says, "except in very unusual cases, no prophet could emerge from an ecstatic experience to give a poetic address couched in such perfect literary form as are the best preserved oracles of Amos, Hosea, and Isaiah."[2] Two of those who have written extensively on this matter of religious experience, Lindblom and Heschel, have gone off in different directions. Lindblom gives much attention to the phenomenon of ecstasy. He rejects a distinction between classical and early prophets on the basis of the presence or absence of ecstasy, rightly noting that the classical prophets are not without ecstatic aspects. One can point out, for example, that Micah claims to be filled with the spirit (Mic 3:8) and that Ezekiel manifests ecstatic traits. However, it is clear that he understands the term very broadly; any sort of vision or audition (or, I suppose, communication of the divine) he sees as evidence of ecstasy.[3]

Heschel's approach is very different. He does not start out with the broader phenomenon of religious experience as Lindblom does. Instead, after an introductory chapter, he begins at once to deal with individual (classical) prophets. Much later (Chapter 12) he explains their attunement to the divine in terms of their sharing in the pathos of God. In this chapter on "The Theology of Pathos" he asserts that "to the prophet, knowledge of God was fellowship with Him, not attained by syllogism or induction, but by living together"—though he explains that "the culmination of prophetic fellowship with God is insight and unanimity—not union." As a quasi-definition: "pathos denotes, not an idea of goodness, but an outgoing challenge, a dynamic relation between God and man; not mere feeling or passive affection, but an act or attitude composed of various spiritual elements; no mere contemplative survey of the world, but a passionate summons."[4] Here Heschel is speaking of *God's* pathos; the prophet comes into it, according to Heschel, in that he participates in God's pathos. In a later chapter he takes up the topic of ecstasy; more precisely, he distinguishes between ecstasy (which means being outside of oneself—*ekstasis*) and enthusiasm (which means being possessed by a god—*entheos*). He investigates these phenomena especially in Greek and Roman sources and denies they are what we find in Israel's prophets.[5] Heschel's discussion is enlightening, though his rejection of ecstasy as an element of Israelite prophecy is at the expense of ignoring the early prophets (from whom, we insist, the classical prophets developed) and the evidence, mentioned above, with reference to Micah and Ezekiel. Nevertheless, his theory of pathos is important in pointing to a significant source of prophetic ethical teaching: the prophet who is in tune with God's outlook on the world, who enjoys fellowship with God, perceives right and wrong in a way not wholly dependent on existing laws and customs.

The religious experience of the classical prophets, at least of the sort described in vocation narratives and in others they occasionally describe, is, in my view, something other than ecstaticism of the sort manifested in the charismatic groups. The ecstatic state can be induced in a number of ways; some groups, in addition to the singing and dancing referred to by Albright, use alcohol or narcotics. Thus there need be nothing supernatural about it or about "communications" received in such ecstasy. Lindblom wants to use the term "ecstasy" but is at pains to explain that it is not the sort "in which the *ego* fully loses consciousness of itself and becomes completely absorbed in the Divine, in the so-called *unio mystica*." He thinks of it rather as "denoting a mental state in which human consciousness is so concentrated on a particular idea or feeling that the normal current of thoughts and perceptions is broken off and the senses temporarily cease to function in a normal way." In rejecting the idea of *unio mystica* he is concerned to preserve the "personal character of prophetic religion" and says "they share in Yahweh's wrath and love and felt themselves bound to His will, because He has laid hold upon them."[6] In such an expression he is not far from the position in which Heschel speaks of the prophet sharing in the "pathos" of God, which sharing Heschel calls "sympathy." Heschel refers to "the inner personal identification of the prophet with the divine pathos," with a strong emphasis on the personal, emotional aspect: "he is convulsed by [the divine pathos] to the depths of his soul."[7] While there is little evidence in the prophets that would justify speaking of "mystical union," it may be asked whether the experiences of the great mystics such as Teresa of Avila or John of the Cross militate in any way against "personal religion"; the writings they have left us certainly do not favor that impression. Perhaps the experience of the classical prophets is comparable to that described by St. Paul when he was "caught up to the third heaven," not knowing whether in or out of the body, and received "visions and revelations of the Lord" (2 Cor 12:2, 1). The kind

of experience we find in the great saints and mystics supposes a high level of prayer, attunement to God, union with God, ability to receive and communicate revelation, and neither requires nor rules out ecstatic aspects.

Mission To Be Bearers of God's Word

Although the early prophets certainly understood themselves to be bearers of God's word, they did not seem to think that was enough, and so we find them involved in revolts, coups d'état, harem intrigues, etc. Somehow they felt themselves compelled to take matters into their own hands, but by that same token they ran the risk of taking them out of God's hands. In the classical prophets, on the other hand, we find more emphasis on the word. Jeremiah is told that he has been set "over nations and over kingdoms" and that he is to "root up and to tear down, / to destroy and to demolish, / to build and to plant" (Jer 1:10), but the only means he is given for this ambitious program is the word of God that had been placed in his mouth, a word he compares to a fire and to a hammer shattering rocks (23:29). And Deutero-Isaiah speaks of the word of the Lord that stands (i.e., prevails, is effective) forever (Isa 40:8), which returns not empty but accomplishes all for which it is sent (55:11). The prophet's word may have political implications, he may attempt to influence policy by carrying the word before kings and people, and he may reinforce it with symbolic acts (as, e.g., in Isaiah 20; Jer 13:1–11; 19:1–13; 27:1–11; Ezekiel 4; 5; etc.), but he does not feel the need to engage in intrigues to bring it to pass. All that is to be done will be accomplished through the word, which, because it *is* the word of the Lord, is supremely efficacious.[8]

Depths of Content of Teaching

Speaking of the early prophets, Albright says: "At first sight it is curious that practically no oracles have survived; what we have belongs to the category of Deuteronomic sermon, though it presumably rests on a traditional nucleus. The prophets of the ecstatic period were men of deeds, not men of words, and the ecstatic tradition was still too strong to be broken."[9] We may question the emphasis given to ecstaticism as the reason, but the fact is that we have nothing from the early prophets that can compare with the collections of oracles of the classical prophets; what we have are mainly threats against this or that king, usually fleshed out by the deuteronomists. If there had been oracles worth preserving, they would have been preserved. On the other hand, we often have extensive narratives about them; this is especially the case with Elijah and Elisha. With the classical prophets we may know very little of their lives and deeds (Jeremiah is by all means the exception), but it is clearly their words that count most. They form perhaps the most important part of the Old Testament and have profoundly influenced the history of the world and its literature (including the New Testament).

Notes

1. This raises the question of whether Amos and the other canonical prophets would have acknowledged the title *nābî*. Joseph Blenkinsopp points out that the canonical prophets refer "almost always disparagingly" to a class of people that call themselves *nebî'îm*, which leads us to wonder whether they would have wished to be known by that title. It has been suggested that the prophetic designation has been added to the canonical books at a later time (*A History of Prophecy* [Louisville: John Knox, 1996] 9).

2. William F. Albright, *From the Stone Age to Christianity* (Garden City, NY: Doubleday, 1957 [c1942]) 306.

3. Johannes Lindblom, *Prophecy in Ancient Israel* (Philadelphia: Fortress, 1965): "A real vision is always based on ecstasy of one form or another" (p. 107).

4. Abraham Joshua Heschel, *The Prophets* (New York: Harper & Row, 1962) 224.

5. *The Prophets*, chs. 19–21, pp. 324–66.

6. *Prophecy in Ancient Israel*, 106. His concern about preserving the personal character of prophetic religion comes strongly to the fore in "Additional Note I" (pp. 423–24), where he discusses in detail scholars who are on one side or the other of the "ecstasy" question.

7. *The Prophets*, 307–08.

8. Brevard S. Childs, *Biblical Theology in Crisis* (Philadelphia: Westminster, 1970) 101, warns of the danger of judging the prophet's experience by our own, of reducing the prophets to our own size by taking the prophet's "hear the word of the Lord" to mean (as we perhaps would mean, since we do not share their experience) "this is what I as a sensitive religious person think."

9. *From the Stone Age to Christianity*, 306.

Joseph Jensen, OSB, *Ethical Dimensions of the Prophet* (Collegeville, MN: Liturgical Press, 2006), 61–66.

Joseph Jensen, OSB, taught scripture for many years. He is the author of several articles and books, including God's Word to Israel.

2. Pre-exilic Prophets: Overview

AMOS

Dates: ca. 760–750 BC

Situation: Amos, a native of Tekoa in the Southern Kingdom of Judah, prophesied in the Northern Kingdom of Israel. Israel experienced prosperity under the rule of King Uzziah and King Jeroboam II, but a disparity existed between the rich and the poor, who were being exploited. Assyria was growing in power and threatened other nations in the region.

Call: Amos was not a professional prophet. He was called by God from his former way of life as a herdsman and a dresser of sycamore trees to be a prophet of the LORD (Amos 7:14–15).

Themes:
- Day of the LORD as a day of judgment, darkness, and gloom (Amos 5:18–20; 8:9–10)
- Empty worship as a symptom of complacency and self-satisfaction resulting from the spiritual decay of the people (Amos 5:21–27; 8:4–6)
- Judgment against Israel (Amos 3–4; 7:1–9)
- Oracles against the nations (Amos 1:3—2:16)
- Remnant presented in the form of a threat, that is, all that will remain after God's judgment are scattered fragments of a people, to whom the LORD may be gracious if they turn from wickedness (Amos 3:12; 5:3, 15)
- Social justice connected to basic human rights, religious observance, and the very spirit of the covenant (Amos 2:6–8; 4:1; 5:10–15; 6:4–6; 8:4–6)

HOSEA

Dates: ca. 750–730 BC

Situation: Hosea, a northern prophet, began to prophesy during the relatively prosperous reign of Jeroboam II. He continued his prophetic activity during the politically chaotic era following Jeroboam's death and leading up to the destruction of Israel by Assyria in 722/21 BC.

Call: Hosea was called by God to be a prophet by taking a harlot as a wife and thus empathizing with the LORD in his experience of rejection, infidelity, and restoring love (Hos 1:1–2; 3:1).

Themes:
- Covenant virtues (righteousness, justice, steadfast love, mercy, faithfulness, and knowledge of the LORD) as bridal gifts bestowed on Israel by God (Hos 2:19–20 [2:21–22 NAB and NJB])
- Exodus/desert experience as a time of Israel's fidelity and an image of future restoration (Hos 2:14–15 [2:16–17 NAB and NJB]; 11:1)
- God as a loving parent (Hos 11:1–4, 8–11)
- Idolatry, offering sacrifice to the Baals and burning incense to idols made by human hands, described as harlotry (Hos 4:12–19; 11:2; 13:2–3)
- Judgment against Israel for participating in empty cult and insincere repentance instead of faithfully loving God (Hos 5:1–15; 6:4–11)
- Marriage as a metaphor for covenant fidelity/infidelity (Hos 1:2—3:5)
- Repentance as sincere conversion and acknowledgement of the LORD's unfathomable and regenerative love (Hos 6:1–3; 14:1–9 [14:2–10 NAB and NJB])
- Symbolic names that signify God's judgment against Israel (Hos 1:4–10 [1:3–8 NAB and NJB]) and God's salvation (Hos 2:1 [2:3 NAB and NJB])

ISAIAH OF JERUSALEM (ISAIAH 1–39)

Dates: ca. 742–700 BC

Situation: Isaiah of Jerusalem (First Isaiah), prophesied in Judah during the reigns of Ahaz and Hezekiah, a turbulent time marked by the Syro-Ephraimaic War (734–732 BC), the fall of the Northern Kingdom of Israel to the Assyrians (722/21 BC), and the Assyrian siege of Jerusalem (701 BC).

Call: Called in the year that king Uzziah died (742 BC) to prophesy in Jerusalem and Judah, Isaiah of Jerusalem had a profound experience of God as the holy one, the king, and the LORD of hosts. He received a mission to deliver a divine message that would not be heeded (Isa 6:1–10).

Themes:

- Davidic covenant as a source of hope in the promise of God to sustain the Davidic line (Isa 37:35)
- Empty worship as characteristic of a people who engage in religious observances, but whose hearts are far from God and whose evil deeds oppress the defenseless (Isa 1:11–18; 29:13–14)
- Holiness as God's special divine characteristic and Isaiah's principal experience of the LORD (Isa 1:4c; 6:1–4)
- Infidelity as being estranged from the Holy One and turning to social injustice (Isa 1:2–4, 21–23)
- Jerusalem/Zion, purified by the judgment of the LORD, will draw the nations to receive God's word and be the source of divine blessing and protection for the faithful (Isa 1:8, 21–26; 2:1–4; 4:2–6; 28:15–16)
- Messianic promise/future hope for a just and righteous Davidic king upon whom the spirit of the LORD shall rest and whose reign will be distinguished by peace, harmony, abundance, and the presence of God (Isa 7:14–15; 9:2–7 [9:1–6 NAB and NJB]; 11:1–10; 35:1–10)
- Remnant from both Israel and Judah as survivors whose return to their land will be accomplished by the zeal of the LORD (Isa 1:9; 9:7 [9:6 NAB and NJB]; 10:20–22; 37:31–32)
- Social justice as connected to religious observance; injustice that elicits judgment by God (Isa 1:15–23; 3:13–15; 5:7–9, 20–23; 10:1–2; 32:5–8)
- Symbolic names indicating what the LORD will do depending on God's disposition toward Israel (Isa 7:3, 14; 8:1–4)
- Trust in the LORD who is Israel's strength and salvation rather than in political and military alliances (Isa 7:4, 9b; 12:2; 30:1–5, 15, 18; 31:1–3; 33:2; 35:3–4)

MICAH OF MORESHETH

Dates: ca. 727–700 BC

Situation: A contemporary of Isaiah, Micah viewed the problems of the day from the perspective of the rural countryside rather than the city of Jerusalem.

Themes:
- Covenant lawsuit as a literary technique in which God puts Israel on trial and, speaking as both prosecutor and judge, defends his position by recalling mighty saving acts carried out on Israel's behalf (Mic 6:1–8)
- Hope of a future restoration of Jerusalem and God's people (Mic 4), as well as the messianic promise of a Davidic king who will come from Bethlehem (Mic 5:2–5a [5:1–4a NAB and NJB])
- Judgment against the leaders, priests, professional prophets (Mic 1–3), and people of Judah for their lack of the moral integrity demanded by the covenant (Mic 6:1—7:6)
- Remnant as a people, including those formerly cast off, who will be lifted above their enemies and ruled and guided by the LORD (Mic 2:12–13; 4:6–7; 5:7–8 [5:6–7 NAB and NJB])
- Social justice connected to faithfulness to God and the covenant (Mic 2:1–2, 8–10; 3:1–3, 9–11; 6:8)

ZEPHANIAH

Dates: ca. 640–625 BC

Situation: Prophesying early in Josiah's reign, Zephaniah addressed the need for reforms following the abuses that developed during the reign of Manasseh (see 2 Kings 21:2–17).

Themes:
- Day of the LORD as a day of universal judgment and destruction, a day of catastrophe for all (Zeph 1:7–18)
- Idolatry, in particular worship of Baal and heavenly bodies (Zeph 1:4–6; 3:1–5)
- Judgment against Judah and Jerusalem (Zeph 1:4–18; 3:1–5)
- Oracles against the nations (Zeph 2)
- Remnant as a people who are humble and lowly, seek refuge in the LORD, are not deceitful, and will be at peace (Zeph 3:12–13)

NAHUM

Dates: ca. 615–612 BC

Situation: Nahum announced the imminent destruction of Nineveh and end of the hated oppressor, Assyria.

Themes:
- Justice of God (Nah 1:2–8)
- Oracles against Assyria and Nineveh (Nah 2:3—3:19 [2:4—3:19 NAB and NJB])

JEREMIAH

Dates: ca. 627-582 BC

Situation: Jeremiah's long prophetic ministry witnessed the end of Assyrian power and the rise of Babylon's dominance. He began prophesying during the reign of Josiah, but the bulk of his prophetic oracles come from the chaotic time after the death of Josiah leading up to the destruction of Jerusalem and the beginning of the exile in Babylon in 587/86 BC.

Call: God appointed Jeremiah a prophet to the nations before his birth and called him during the thirteenth year of the reign of King Josiah (627 BC). The LORD placed the divine message in the prophet's mouth and commissioned Jeremiah, setting him "over nations and over kingdoms, to pluck up and to break down, to destroy and to overthrow, to build and to plant" (Jer 1:4-10).

Themes:
- Confessions/laments of Jeremiah provide insights into his relationship with the LORD and into his personal anguish as a prophet in service to the word of God (Jer 11:18—12:6; 15:10-21; 17:14-18; 18:18-23; 20:7-13; 20:14-18)
- Covenant infidelity as the reason for God's acts of judgment against Judah and Jerusalem (Jer 11:1-17)
- Future hope for the mercy of God, the reign of righteous Davidic kings, the restoration of Israel and Judah, and a new covenant (Jer 23:5-8; 29:10-14; 30:1—33:26)
- Idolatry as a great sin of Judah, which calls for God's corrective judgment (Jer 2:4-28; 10:2-5)
- Ineradicable nature of Judah's sin (Jer 13:23; 17:1)
- Judgment against Judah and Jerusalem in the form of the destruction of the cities of Judah, including Jerusalem, by the Babylonians (Jer 10:22; 21:8-10)
- New covenant made with the house of Israel through which God's law is written upon the people's hearts and God is known because of divine forgiveness (Jer 31:31-37)
- Social justice as connected to God's blessings and judgment on Judah (Jer 5:26-28; 7:5-6; 21:12)
- Symbolic actions used as a means for communicating the prophetic message (Jer 13:1-11; 16:1-13; 18:1-11; 19:1-14; 27:1—28:17; 32:6-15)
- Temple sermon as a summary of God's complaint against the complacency and spiritual decay of the people, the divine call to conversion, and the LORD's promise of judgment if there is no repentance (Jer 7:1-15; 26:1-6)
- Warning against heeding the message of false prophets who fill the people with vain hopes (Jer 6:13-14; 14:13-16; 23:16-17; 27:14-18; 28:1-17)
- Images of wounds/healing used to describe the condition of the prophet and God's people, as well as the action of the LORD on their behalf (Jer 3:22; 6:14; 8:22; 10:19; 14:17-19; 17:14; 30:17)

3. *The Jewish People and Their Sacred Scriptures in the Christian Bible, §21*

The Pontifical Biblical Commission, 2002

The Unity of God's Plan and the Idea of Fulfillment

21. The basic theological presupposition is that God's salvific plan which culminates in Christ (cf. Eph 1:3–14) is a unity, but that it is realized progressively over the course of time. Both the unity and the gradual realization are important; likewise, continuity in certain points and discontinuity in others. From the outset, the action of God regarding human beings has tended towards final fulfillment and, consequently, certain aspects that remain constant began to appear: God reveals himself, calls, confers a mission, promises, liberates, makes a covenant. The first realizations, though provisional and imperfect, already give a glimpse of the final plenitude. This is particularly evident in certain important themes which are developed throughout the entire Bible, from Genesis to Revelation: the way, the banquet, God's dwelling among men. Beginning from a continuous re-reading of events and texts, the Old Testament itself progressively opens up a perspective of fulfillment that is final and definitive. The Exodus, the primordial experience of Israel's faith (cf. Deut 6:20–25; 26:5–9) becomes the symbol of final salvation. Liberation from the Babylonian Exile and the prospect of an eschatological salvation are described as a new Exodus.[41] Christian interpretation is situated along these lines with this difference, that the fulfillment is already substantially realized in the mystery of Christ.

The notion of fulfillment is an extremely complex one,[42] one that could easily be distorted if there is a unilateral insistence either on continuity or discontinuity. Christian faith recognizes the fulfillment, in Christ, of the Scriptures and the hopes of Israel, but it does not understand this fulfillment as a literal one. Such a conception would be reductionist. In reality, in the mystery of Christ crucified and risen, fulfillment is brought about in a manner unforeseen. It includes transcendence.[43] Jesus is not confined to playing an already fixed role—that of Messiah—but he confers, on the notions of Messiah and salvation, a fullness which could not have been imagined in advance; he fills them with a new reality; one can even speak in this connection of a "new creation."[44] It would be wrong to consider the prophecies of the Old Testament as some kind of photographic anticipations of future events. All the texts, including those which later were read as messianic prophecies, already had an immediate import and meaning for their contemporaries before attaining a fuller meaning for future hearers. The messiahship of Jesus has a meaning that is new and original.

The original task of the prophet was to help his contemporaries understand the events and the times they lived in from God's viewpoint. Accordingly, excessive insistence, characteristic of a certain apologetic, on the probative value attributable to the fulfillment of prophecy must be discarded. This insistence has contributed to harsh judgments by Christians of Jews and their reading of the Old Testament: the more reference to

Christ is found in Old Testament texts, the more the incredulity of the Jews is considered inexcusable and obstinate.

Insistence on discontinuity between both Testaments and going beyond former perspectives should not, however, lead to a one-sided spiritualization. What has already been accomplished in Christ must yet be accomplished in us and in the world. The definitive fulfillment will be at the end with the resurrection of the dead, a new heaven and a new earth. Jewish messianic expectation is not in vain. It can become for us Christians a powerful stimulant to keep alive the eschatological dimension of our faith. Like them, we too live in expectation. The difference is that for us the One who is to come will have the traits of the Jesus who has already come and is already present and active among us.

Current Perspectives

The Old Testament in itself has great value as the Word of God. To read the Old Testament as Christians then does not mean wishing to find everywhere direct reference to Jesus and to Christian realities. True, for Christians, all the Old Testament economy is in movement towards Christ; if then the Old Testament is read in the light of Christ, one can, retrospectively, perceive something of this movement. But since it is a movement, a slow and difficult progression throughout the course of history, each event and each text is situated at a particular point along the way, at a greater or lesser distance from the end.

Retrospective re-readings through Christian eyes mean perceiving both the movement towards Christ and the distance from Christ, prefiguration and dissimilarity. Conversely, the New Testament cannot be fully understood except in the light of the Old Testament.

The Christian interpretation of the Old Testament is then a differentiated one, depending on the different genres of texts. It does not blur the difference between Law and Gospel, but distinguishes carefully the successive phases of revelation and salvation history. It is a theological interpretation, but at the same time historically grounded. Far from excluding historical-critical exegesis, it demands it.

Although the Christian reader is aware that the internal dynamism of the Old Testament finds its goal in Jesus, this is a retrospective perception whose point of departure is not in the text as such, but in the events of the New Testament proclaimed by the apostolic preaching. It cannot be said, therefore, that Jews do not see what has been proclaimed in the text, but that the Christian, in the light of Christ and in the Spirit, discovers in the text an additional meaning that was hidden there.

Notes

41. Isa 35:1–10; 40:1–5; 43:1–22; 48:12–21; 62.
42. Cf. below II B.9 and C, nos 54-65.
43. "Non solum impletur, verum etiam transcenditur", Ambroise Autpert, quoted by H. de Lubac, *Exégèse médiévale*, II.246.
44. 2 Co 5:17; Ga 6:15.

4. The Prism of Sennacherib, iii 18–49

(An Assyrian Account of the Siege of Jerusalem)

Sennacherib, 704–681 BC

The Siege of Jerusalem

As to Hezekiah, the Jew, he did not submit to my yoke, I laid siege to 46 of his strong cities, walled forts and to the countless small villages in their vicinity, and conquered (them) by means of well-stamped (earth-) ramps, and battering-rams brought (thus) near (to the walls) (combined with) the attack by foot soldiers, (using) mines, breeches as well as sapper work. I drove out (of them) 200, 150 people, young and old, male and female, horses, mules, donkeys, camels, big and small cattle beyond counting, and considered (them) booty. Himself I made a prisoner in Jerusalem, his royal residence, like a bird in a cage, I surrounded him with earthwork in order to molest those who were leaving his city's gate. His towns which I had plundered, I took away from his country and gave them (over) to Mitinti, king of Ashdod, Padi, king of Ekron, and Sillibel,

king of Gaza. Thus I reduced his country, but I still increased the tribute and the *katrû*-presents (due) to me (as his) overlord which I imposed (later) upon him beyond the former tribute, to be delivered annually. Hezekiah himself, whom the terror-inspiring splendor of my lordship had overwhelmed and whose irregular and elite troops which he had brought into Jerusalem, his royal residence, in order to strengthen (it), had deserted him, did send me, later, to Nineveh, my lordly city, together with 30 talents of gold, 800 talents of silver, precious stones, antimony, large cuts of red stone, couches (inlaid) with ivory, *nimedu*-chairs (in-laid) with ivory, elephant-hides, ebony-wood, box-wood (and) all kinds of valuable treasures, his (own) daughters, concubines, male and female musicians. In order to deliver the tribute and to do obeisance as a slave he sent his (personal) messenger.

From *Ancient Near Eastern Texts*, ed. James B. Prichard (Princeton, Princeton University Press, 1969), 287–88.

5. Self-Quiz: Mid-Unit One

In the blank before each statement in the first column, place the letter of the prophet in the second column who is BEST described by that statement. A prophet's name may be used more than once.

_____ 1. Married a harlot

_____ 2. Named a child "a remnant shall return"

_____ 3. Proclaimed the birth of Immanuel

_____ 4. Used a good example of a covenant lawsuit

_____ 5. Stressed the Davidic Covenant and the greatness of Mt. Zion/Jerusalem

_____ 6. During his call, he experienced the holiness of God in a vision in the temple

_____ 7. Saw God as lover, faithful spouse, and parent

_____ 8. Saw God's justice in the destruction of Nineveh

_____ 9. Connected universal destruction with the proclamation of the Day of the LORD

_____ 10. Came from Judah, but called for justice in Israel

_____ 11. Looked forward to a ruler/messiah from Bethlehem

_____ 12. Named a child "not my people"

a. Amos

b. Hosea

c. Isaiah of Jerusalem

d. Micah

e. Zephaniah

f. Nahum

(Answers to quiz can be found on page 105.)

6. Self-Quiz: Unit One Maps

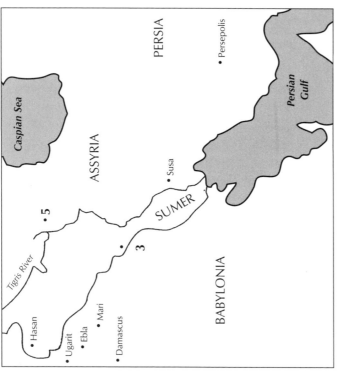

In the blank before each place name, write the number of the location on the maps.

——— a. Anathoth •

——— b. Babylon

——— c. Bethel

——— d. Moresheth

——— e. Nineveh

——— f. Tekoa •

(Answers to quiz can be found on page 105.)

7. The Meaning of the Exile

Eloi Leclerc, OFM

Faith is presently undergoing a very serious crisis. Men and women who have committed their lives to the certainties of faith feel that in their environment and in religious circles themselves, these basic and vital certainties have begun to waver...

What we are called to live today has in fact already been lived in a prophetic way by the people of God at a given moment of its history, precisely during the long exile which followed the national disaster of 587 B.C. This exile, which lasted some fifty years, was a true night crossing for the people of God; it meant the end of an age. The people then experienced the nightfall of their institutions. Everything that formed their framework and protection fell into the shadows. Everything that could give it confidence in its own destiny was destroyed. Jerusalem and its temple were leveled. The kingdom was suppressed, the land occupied and annexed, the elite deported. Stripped of all the special signs that made it the chosen people and dispersed among the pagan nations, Israel was brought back to its primal nakedness. It was driven to face the basic poverty of the person. "Days of darkness and of tumult": this is how the prophet Ezekiel characterized this time of deportation. Israel no longer knew beforehand who the eternal one was or what he wanted. It had to grope through the night. It is not from the flashing mountaintop of Sinai that the saving word comes, but from the depths of a broken heart.

This experience was lived at such a depth that it transcends the particular historical circumstances within which it unfolded. By touching the deepest part of the person, it attains universality. Certain situations were lived and certain words were said which make this moment of biblical history a prophecy of the deep becoming of the person, for each individual as well as for the entire people of God. Because of this, this experience now concerns us directly. Within it is enclosed the only light which can enlighten our current journey through the night by making us see what we ourselves are called to become.

What becomes of a person when he or she has lost everything, even that which he or she held most sacred? How does one then live one's relationship to the world, to others, and to oneself? To which renewal is one called? And by what way? How can the darkest night become a moment of hope? Through what metamorphosis? All these questions we have asked ourselves while meditating on this great moment of torment for the people of God.

The more a human experience is radical the more it can reveal to us what is fundamental and eternal. And the biblical experience of exile is one of the most radical experiences that humanity has ever undergone. No one can go through such distress without falling into a bottomless despair unless one encounters at the bottom of the abyss an indestructible hope. Today the people of God need to encounter such hope.

Eloi LeClerc, OFM, *People of God in the Night* (Chicago: Franciscan Herald Press, 1979), 1, 3–5.

8. Literature of the Exile: Overview

LAMENTATIONS

Date: ca. 587/86 BC

Situation: Written in Jerusalem after its destruction by Babylon, Lamentations is a response to the destruction, suffering, chaos, and struggle for survival of those who remained in the city.

Structure: Five laments in the form of funeral dirges written in chiastic, acrostic form

Themes:
- Call to interior conversion and admission of sin (Lam 3:40–42)
- Hope in the midst of pain (Lam 3:21–33)
- Images of God:
  - Enemy, who is seen as the cause of Jerusalem's suffering (Lam 2:1–8, 17, 22; 3:1–18, 43–45)
  - Just judge, who punishes Jerusalem for her sins (Lam 1:5, 8, 14, 18; 3:37–39; 4:13, 22)
  - Redeemer, whose saving deeds in the past offer hope for similar deeds in the future (Lam 3:55–66)
- Suffering: the acrostic style symbolizes the fullness of suffering and grief

OBADIAH

Date: after 587/86 BC

Situation: Edom assisted the Babylonians in the destruction of Jerusalem.

Theme: An oracle against Edom

EZEKIEL

Dates: ca. 593–573 BC

Situation: Ezekiel, a priest, prophesied to the exiles in Babylon during the early years of the exile.

Call: In his call, which comes to him in a vision, Ezekiel experiences the glory of God. He eats the scroll containing "words of lamentation and mourning and woe" (Ezek 1–3)

Themes:
- Allegories:
  - Israel as God's adulterous wife (Ezek 16)
  - Eagle and the vine alludes to the kings and international issues (Ezek 17)
  - Infidelity of Samaria and Jerusalem (Ezek 23)
  - Siege of Jerusalem is likened to a boiling pot (Ezek 24:3–14)
- Glory/holiness of God, a priestly image (Ezek 1:28; 3:12, 23; 8:4; 10:18–19; 11:22–23; 36:22–23; 43:2–5)
- Images of hope and restoration (Ezek 33–38)
  - Dry bones, symbolizing that Israel, will be brought to life by the spirit of God (Ezek 37:1–14)
  - New heart and spirit, which will enable the people to "follow God's statutes and observe his ordinances" (Ezek 11:19; 36:24–27; 37:14)
  - Shepherding, which the leaders have not done well, so that now God will be the people's shepherd (Ezek 34)
- Individual responsibility; not the sins of the parents, but rather one's own deeds are what count (Ezek 3:16–21; 18)
- "Know that I am the LORD": God acts so that his holy name and his power will be known

(Ezek 11:10, 12; 12:20; 16:62; 20:38, 42, 44; 23:49; 24:24, 27; 33:29; 34:27; 35:9, 15; 36:11, 20–23, 38; 37:6, 13)
- Symbolic prophetic actions are used to dramatize the prophet's message (Ezek 2:8—3:3; 3:25–27; 4:1–17; 5:1–12; 12:1–20; 24:15–24; 33:21–22; 37:15–28)
- The temple is used as an image of both judgment and life-giving restoration (Ezek 8:1—11:24; 43:1–12; 47:1–12)

SECOND ISAIAH (ISAIAH 40–55)

Date: ca. 540 BC

Situation: The prophet, also known as Deutero-Isaiah, prophesied to the exiles shortly before Cyrus, the Persian, conquered the Babylonians and set the stage for the exiles' return to Judah.

Themes:
- Consolation/comfort signaling the end of exile (Isa 40:1–11; 51:12)
- Cyrus of Persia, God's anointed one (Isa 41:2–3, 25; 44:28—45:5)
- Images of God:
  - Creator (Isa 40:12, 21–28; 42:5; 44:24; 45:12, 18; 48:13; 51:13, 16; 54:5a)
  - Compassionate one (Isa 46:3–4; 49:15–16; 54:7–10)
  - The only God (monotheism); idols are nothing (Isa 40:12–31; 41:1–24; 44:6–20; 45:5–7, 18–25)
  - Redeemer (Isa 43:1b; 44:6a, 24a; 48:20; 49:7; 52:9b; 54:5b, 8b)
- Restoration/return:
  - The suffering of Jerusalem/Zion is over (Isa 40:9–11; 51:3–11; 52:1–12; 54:1–10)
  - New exodus: the return from exile will be even greater than the exodus from Egypt (Isa 40:3–5; 43:14–21; 44:17–21; 49:10–11; 55:12–13)
- Servant Songs (Isa 42:1–4; 49:1–6; 50:4–9; 52:13—53:12)
- Word of the LORD (Isa 40:6–8; 55:10–11)

9. Restoration Literature: Overview

HAGGAI

Date: 520 BC

Situation: In the midst of the poverty and chaos following the return from exile, Haggai urged the people of Jerusalem to rebuild the temple.

Themes:
- Rebuilding of the temple (Hag 1:2–11)
- Messianic expectations for Zerubbabel (Hag 2:3–9, 20–23)

FIRST ZECHARIAH (ZECHARIAH 1–8)

Dates: 520–518 BC

Situation: Zechariah, a contemporary of Haggai, addressed the issues of the early post-exilic period through a series of eight visions.

Themes:
- Angels interpret visions (Zech 1:9, 19 [2:1 NAB and NJB]; 2:3[2:7 NAB and NJB]; 3:1, 6; 4:1, 5; 5:5; 6:4–5)
- Call to conversion, a reversal of the sins that led to Jerusalem's destruction (Zech 1:1–6)
- Jerusalem/temple: God's jealousy for Jerusalem and promise to dwell in her; all nations drawn to her (Zech 1:12—2:13 [1:12—2:17 NAB and NJB]; 8:1–17, 20–23)
- Messianic expectations for Joshua the priest and Zerubbabel (Zech 3:8; 4:1–14; 6:9–15)
- Satan, a member of God's council, the accuser (Zech 3:1–2)
- Social justice: reminder that past failure to heed the call to justice led to punishment (Zech 7:8–14; 8:14–17)

THIRD ISAIAH (ISAIAH 56–66)

Date: Probably early post-exilic period

Situation: Third (Trito) Isaiah addressed the problems and hopes of the early post-exilic community in Judah.

Call: The prophet was anointed by the spirit of the LORD (Isa 61:1–3)

Themes:
- Divisions in the community, both social and religious issues cause conflict (Isa 56:9—57:2; 59:1–15; 65:13–16)
- Idolatry as useless, but people continue to fall into it (Isa 57:3–13; 65:1–7)
- Image of God as warrior/redeemer (Isa 59:15b–20; 63:1–6; 66:14–16)
- New Jerusalem/Zion, a promise of blessing and hope (Isa 60:1–22; 61:1–4; 62:1–12; 65:17–25; 66:10–14)
- Social justice tied to religious observance, in particular fasting (Isa 58:1—59:15)
- Universal salvation for all who observe the Sabbath and are faithful to the covenant; even foreigners and eunuchs are welcome in the temple (Isa 56:1–8; 66:18–23)
- Holy Spirit (Isa 63:10)

EZRA

Dates:
- Final editing: late fifth to early fourth century
- Mission of Ezra: ca. 458 BC or ca. 398 BC

Situation: The Book of Ezra covers two different post-exilic periods: first, the return of the exiles, their conflicts with the Samaritans and the people of the land, and the rebuilding of the temple in the sixth century BC (Ezra 1–6); second, the religious reforms of Ezra, the priest and scribe, in the fifth or possibly early fourth century BC (Ezra 7–10).

Themes:
- Continuity with the past, especially with regard to worship (Ezra 1:7–11; 3:2–5, 10–13; 5:11–17; 6:3–5, 18–22; 7:1–6, 10, 13, 27; 8:1–14, 18–20)
- Exclusivity, returned exiles forbid others from joining in the rebuilding of the temple, mixed marriages forbidden, and foreign wives and children sent away (Ezra 4:1–3; 9:1–4, 10–15; 1:1–18, 44)
- People of the land seen in a negative light (Ezra 4:4–5; 9:1–2)
- Temple and cult restored (Ezra 1:2–11; 2:6—3:13; 5:1–17; 6:3–22; 7:7, 15–24; 8:24–30, 33–36)
- Torah observance at the center of Ezra's reforms (Ezra 7:5, 10–12, 14, 25–26)

NEHEMIAH

Dates:
- Final editing: late fifth to early fourth century
- Mission of Nehemiah: last half of the fifth century. Nehemiah served as governor of Judah for twelve years, from 445 to 433 BC, before returning to Persia and then coming back to Judah.

Situation: Nehemiah rebuilt the walls of Jerusalem and dealt with the social and religious abuses that had developed in the post-exilic community.

Themes:
- Covenant renewal conducted by Ezra the priest (Neh 8–10)
- Exclusivity; returnees separate themselves from others, mixed marriages are forbidden (Neh 9:2; 13:1–3; 13:23–27)
- Rebuilding the walls of Jerusalem (Neh 2:5, 11–20; 4 [3:33—4:17 NAB and NJB]; 6:15–16)
- Reforms:
  - Sabbath observance restored (Neh 13:15–22)
  - Social injustice rectified (Neh 5:1—19)
  - Temple abuses ended (Neh 13:4–14, 28–30)
- Prayer is central to all Nehemiah's actions (Neh 1:4–11; 2:4; 4:4–5 [3:36–37 NAB and NJB], 9 [4:3 NAB and NJB]; 5:13, 19; 6:9, 14; 9:5–37; 13:14, 22b, 31b)

10. Self-Quiz: Mid-Unit Two

Match the following statements with the appropriate book (a book may be used more than once):

_____ 1. Prophesied that the return from the exile was imminent

_____ 2. Human suffering from A–Z (acrostic)

_____ 3. Idols are impotent nothings

_____ 4. Individual responsibility for one's own sins

_____ 5. Israel is called Servant of the LORD

_____ 6. Book of consolation

_____ 7. God's presence not limited to the temple; God is also present to the people in exile

_____ 8. Oracles against the Edomites

_____ 9. Encouraged the rebuilding of the temple after the return from exile (give one of two possible answers)

_____ 10. Set in Jerusalem at the time of the fall of the city

_____ 11. Prophesied in Babylon at the beginning of the exile

_____ 12. Saw Cyrus as God's anointed

_____ 13. Explored the theme of suffering as redemptive

_____ 14. Chastised the people for being concerned about their own homes/fields rather than rebuilding the temple

_____ 15. Post-exilic prophecy containing eight visions

a. Lamentations

b. Obadiah

c. Ezekiel

d. Second Isaiah

e. Haggai

f. Zechariah

(Answers to quiz can be found on page 105.)

11. Self-Quiz: Unit Two Map

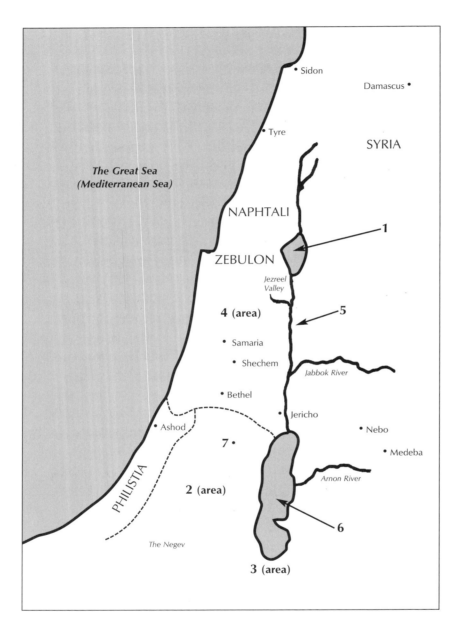

For each place named below, insert the correct number from the map:

_____ a. Dead Sea

_____ b. Edom

_____ c. Jerusalem

_____ d. Jordan River

_____ e. Judah

_____ f. Samaria (area)

_____ g. Sea of Galilee

(Answers to quiz can be found on page 105.)

12. David the King: Two Biblical Portraits

Leslie J. Hoppe, OFM

During the months preceding a presidential election, both the supporters and opponents of a specific candidate will offer their contrasting profiles of the candidate, his or her political philosophy, qualifications for office, and stands on the issues. When one examines the two profiles, one wonders how they can be describing the same person. Supporters will try to present their candidate as combining the best qualities of George Washington and Abraham Lincoln, while opponents will try to show that the candidate makes Millard Fillmore and Warren G. Harding look good! The Bible does something similar to one of the most well-known and beloved biblical characters: David.

On the surface, it appears that the Bible presents a very positive image of David. After all, both Testaments characterize David as a man "after God's own heart" (see 1 Sam 13:14; Acts 13:22). The Old Testament tells several stories about David that have engaged the imagination of readers over the millennia. Who does not know the story of David and Goliath (1 Samuel 17)—a tale of a great victory against very long odds? Similarly, one is hard pressed to find a more charming story of friendship than that of David and Jonathan—a story woven through 1 Samuel and crowned by David's touchingly beautiful elegy for Jonathan and Saul when he learns of their deaths (2 Sam 1:17–27). The New Testament also includes numerous references to David. The Synoptic Gospels present Jesus as the "son of David." Indeed, the New Testament begins with Matthew's genealogy of "Jesus Christ, the son of David" (Matt 1:1). Both Matthew and Luke have Jesus born in Bethlehem,

"the city of David" (Matt 2:1; Luke 2:4). Still, a careful reading of the Bible reveals a dark side to this beloved character.

David in the Former Prophets

David's story takes up a sizable portion of the books that the ancient rabbis named the Former Prophets and modern scholars term the Deuteronomistic history of Israel (Joshua, Judges, Samuel, and Kings). These books tell the story of Israel in its land from the miraculous entrance of the Israelite tribes into Canaan under Joshua to the tragic exile of the people of Judah and Jerusalem from that land under Nebuchadnezzar. David makes his first appearance in this story when God sends Samuel to Bethlehem where the prophet found the person God chose to replace Saul as king (1 Sam 16:1). It is not until 1 Kings 2 that David's story ends with the notice of his death and burial (1 Kgs 2:10–11). Even after death, David does not disappear from the Former Prophets. His memory is evoked more than fifty times in the rest of the story of Israel in its land. He receives by far the most attention of any character in the Deuteronomistic history.

The Deuteronomist's story of David begins well enough. It is an Horatio Alger tale that many readers find appealing. The books of Samuel follow the rise of a simple shepherd boy to the throne of a great kingdom. The lad whose sole responsibility was his father's sheep came to rule over territories that stretched from the Euphrates to the Sinai, from the Mediterranean to the Transjordan (see 2 Sam 24:4–7). But David's rise to kingship was full of peril. He had to deal with Saul maddened by jealousy, the Philistines' desire to take Israel's land, and the loyalty of some Israelites to the house of Saul. In the end, he overcame every obstacle and ascended the throne. The Deuteronomist uses the story of Nathan's oracle (2 Samuel 7) to assert God's approval on David's rise to royal power. Still, there are intimations that David is not the unsullied hero that popular imagination made him out to be.

Rise to Power

The books of Samuel present David as carefully orchestrating his rise to power. He marries into Saul's family (1 Sam 18:17–29). He takes two other wives from influential families—one from the south and one from the north (1 Sam 25:39–43). He escapes from Saul by allying himself with the Philistines (1 Samuel 27). He puts the elders of Judah into his debt by sharing with them the booty gained from his raids (30:26–31). He cuts a deal with Abner who was a supporter of Ishbaal, Saul's surviving son (2 Samuel 3). He takes possession of the ark of the covenant, an important Israelite religious symbol (2 Samuel 6). David decides to build a temple for Yahweh (2 Sam 7:1–2). Now the building of a temple was a royal prerogative, so the project David had in mind was an attempt to provide religious support for his succession to Saul as king. Finally, David "invites" Meribbaal (Mephi-bosheth), the last survivor of the house of Saul, to live in the palace with him, thus neutralizing the last possible threat to his legitimacy as king (2 Samuel 9). David, however, made a serious—almost fatal—misstep that undermined all his efforts to secure his place as king.

The story of David's involvement with Bathsheba marks an abrupt change in David's fortunes. The Bathsheba affair was no mere dalliance; rather, it followed David's pattern of marrying women from influential families as a way to shore

up his position as king. But Bathsheba was already married when David met her. David faced the same problem when he decided to marry Abigail, but her husband Nabal died, thus opening the way for David to wed his very wealthy widow (1 Sam 25:36–42). This time, however, it was different, so David arranged for Uriah, Bathsheba's husband, to be placed in harm's way during the siege of Rabbah (2 Sam 11:14–17). Uriah's death enabled David to add Bathsheba to his growing harem. But the marriage did not have its intended effect. Far from shoring up support for David, it began a downward spiral that nearly consumed David's entire family.

Downward Spiral

The first to be caught up in the disastrous effects of David's sins was the most innocent of all: the first child that Bathsheba bore for David (2 Sam 12:15). The infant died shortly after birth. David's life was spared because he acknowledged his sin and repented when confronted by the prophet Nathan (2 Sam 12:13–14). Still, there seemed to be a curse hanging above David's family. First, Amnon, David's eldest son, raped Tamar, his half-sister (2 Sam 13:1–22). David did nothing in the face of this terrible crime so Absalom, David's third son and Tamar's full brother, avenged this outrage by killing Amnon. To be safe from his father's anger, Absalom fled to the court of his maternal grandfather Talmai, the king of Geshur, located in what is now known as the Golan Heights (2 Sam 13:23–37). David could do nothing but mourn the loss of two sons: one a victim of fratricide and the other an exile. After three years, David was persuaded to guarantee Absalom's safety, making it possible for his son to return from exile. But the breach between father and son was not healed; David refused to see his son for two years after his return from Geshur (2 Sam 14:24–28). For his part, Absalom could not forget David's failure to discipline Amnon for the rape of Tamar. This resentment led Absalom to subvert his father's rule and then to engage in overt rebellion that forced David to flee for his life (2 Samuel 15-16). Absalom failed to press his initial advantage, and his revolt failed. Joab, one of David's generals, killed Absalom, and David was plunged into grief by the death of yet another son (2 Samuel 18). David's prolonged mourning over Absalom led to a vacuum of power in Jerusalem, though eventually David reclaimed his position as king (2 Samuel 19-20). But he was never the same person again.

The final act in the disintegration of David's family was the unseemly intrigue between his sons Adonijah and Solomon over the succession to the throne (1 Kings 1-2). Each laid claim to that throne while David was still alive. Solomon was successful in finding popular support for his claim but still found it necessary to kill his brother to ensure the succession. The end of David's story portrayed him as feeble and ineffectual. David was no longer shaping events; he was reduced to reacting to events shaped by others. It was a sad ending to a story that [had begun] with so much promise.

David in the Books of Chronicles

The portrait of David found in the Chronicler's story of Israel is quite different from that in the Former Prophets. The Chronicler implies that Israel's story really began with David. The first nine chapters of 1 Chronicles contain nothing but genealogies—no narratives at all. Chapter 10 gives Saul some attention, but his story only serves to introduce that of David, which takes up chapters 11-29. David, then, is the major character in 1 Chronicles—but it is a David quite different from the figure depicted in 1-2 Samuel. The Chronicler omits the story of David's rise to power with its description of the steps that David took to ensure his succession to Saul's throne. Also suppressed is

the story of the Bathsheba affair with its most unflattering portrait of David. Similarly unmentioned is the disintegration of David's family.

The Chronicler portrays David as devoting his entire attention and energy to preparing for the building of the future Temple. David had stonecutters dressing the stones that eventually became part of the temple structure. He amassed vast quantities of iron, wood, and other materials necessary for erecting the building, and he charged Solomon with overseeing the construction (1 Chronicles 22), giving him the plans for the arrangement of rooms in the building's interior and a list of its furnishings (1 Chr 28:11-18). David organized the administration of the Temple, appointing officers, gatekeepers, and musicians (1 Chr 23:4-5). The Chronicler noted that it was David who appointed Asaph to compose psalms and provided an example of one such psalm (16:8-36). Most important of all, he made arrangements for the priests and Levites to preside over the worship in the Temple (1 Chronicles 23-24). The king provided for the adornment of the building out of his personal fortune and encouraged the wealthy to do the same (29:1-9). David's last words were a prayer that Solomon [might] build the Temple and a charge to all Israel to "bless the LORD" (29:19-20). The Chronicler depicts David as completely devoted to God as evidenced by all that he did to prepare for the future Temple—a picture of David that is very different from that found in the Former Prophets.

Why Two Portraits?

The differences between the Deuteronomist's and the Chronicler's portraits of David are too extreme and too obvious to be glossed over. How could both authors have been describing the same person? Perhaps those responsible for translating the Hebrew Bible into Greek had this question in mind when they gave a Greek name to the books of

Chronicles. The Septuagint calls these books *Paralipomenon,* "that which was left out" (from the books of Samuel and Kings). But that is too easy a solution to the problem of finding some common ground between the two dissimilar biblical portraits of David. Despite the ample differences between them, the Deuteronomistic and Chronistic portraits of David both see David as a "larger than life" figure. For both works, David is Israel in miniature.

For the Deuteronomist, David represents Israel at its worst. What began with so much promise ends in tragedy because of sin. The only glimmer of hope comes with David's life being spared when he admits his sin [after being] confronted by Nathan (2 Sam 12:13). For the Chronicler, David represents Israel at its best—when it devotes itself entirely to the worship of its God. The Chronicler sees Israel's future as bound up with the service of Yahweh. Christian readers can appropriate these two very different portraits of David by identifying themselves with David as the Deuteronomist and the Chronicler suggest.

The Church's future is a consequence not simply of its sinful past but especially of its commitment to the service of God

Suggestions for Further Reading

Walter Brueggemann. *David's Truth in Israel's Imagination and Memory.* Philadelphia: Fortress Press, 1985.

David M. Gunn. *The Story of David.* Sheffield: Sheffield Academic Press, 1978.

Stephen L. McKenzie. *King David: A Biography.* New York: Oxford University Press, 2000.

Leslie J. Hoppe, OFM, "David the King: Two Biblical Portraits," *The Bible Today* 42, 3 (2004): 137–42.

Leslie J. Hoppe, OFM, is provincial minister of the Assumption Province Franciscans. He is also an adjunct professor of Old Testament studies at Catholic Theological Union.

13. Synoptic Comparison 1: The Bringing of the Ark to Jerusalem

2 Samuel 6:1–23	1 Chronicles 13:1—16:7
No parallel	**13** [1]David consulted with the commanders of the thousands and of the hundreds, with every leader. [2]David said to the whole assembly of Israel, "If it seems good to you, and if it is the will of the Lord our God, let us send abroad to our kindred who remain in all the land of Israel, including the priests and Levites in the cities that have pasture lands, that they may come together to us. [3]Then let us bring again the ark of our God to us; for we did not turn to it in the days of Saul." [4]The whole assembly agreed to do so, for the thing pleased all the people.
6:1–11	13:5–14
5:11–25	14:1–16
No parallel	**15** [1]David built houses for himself in the city of David, and he prepared a place for the ark of God and pitched a tent for it. [2]Then David commanded that no one but the Levites were to carry the ark of God, for the LORD had chosen them to carry the ark of the LORD and to minister to him for ever. [3]David assembled all Israel in Jerusalem to bring up the ark of the LORD to its place, which he had prepared for it. [4]Then David gathered together the descendants of Aaron and the Levites: [5]of the sons of Kohath, Uriel the chief, with one hundred and twenty of his kindred; [6]of the sons of Merari, Asaiah the chief, with two hundred and twenty of his kindred; [7]of the sons of Gershom, Joel the chief, with one hundred and thirty of his kindred; [8]of the sons of Elizaphan, Shemaiah the chief, with two hundred of his kindred; [9]of the sons of Hebron, Eliel the chief, with eighty of his kindred;

¹⁰of the sons of Uzziel, Amminadab the chief, with one hundred and twelve of his kindred. ¹¹David summoned the priests Zadok and Abiathar, and the Levites Uriel, Asaiah, Joel, Shemaiah, Eliel, and Amminadab. ¹²He said to them, "You are the heads of families of the Levites; sanctify yourselves, you and your kindred, so that you may bring up the ark of the LORD, the God of Israel, to the place that I have prepared for it. ¹³Because you did not carry it the first time, the Lord our God burst out against us, because we did not give it proper care." ¹⁴So the priests and the Levites sanctified themselves to bring up the ark of the LORD, the God of Israel. ¹⁵And the Levites carried the ark of God on their shoulders with the poles, as Moses had commanded according to the word of the LORD.

¹⁶David also commanded the chiefs of the Levites to appoint their kindred as the singers to play on musical instruments, on harps and lyres and cymbals, to raise loud sounds of joy. ¹⁷So the Levites appointed Heman son of Joel; and of his kindred Asaph son of Berechiah; and of the sons of Merari, their kindred, Ethan son of Kushaiah; ¹⁸and with them their kindred of the second order, Zechariah, Jaaziel, Shemiramoth, Jehiel, Unni, Eliab, Benaiah, Maaseiah, Mattithiah, Eliphelehu, and Mikneiah, and the gatekeepers Obed-edom and Jeiel. ¹⁹The singers Heman, Asaph, and Ethan were to sound bronze cymbals; ²⁰Zechariah, Aziel, Shemiramoth, Jehiel, Unni, Eliab, Maaseiah, and Benaiah were to play harps according to Alamoth; ²¹but Mattithiah, Eliphelehu, Mikneiah, Obed-edom, Jeiel, and Azaziah were to lead with lyres according to the Sheminith. ²²Chenaniah, leader of the Levites in music, was to direct the music, for he understood it. ²³Berechiah and Elkanah were to be gatekeepers for the ark. ²⁴Shebaniah, Joshaphat, Nethanel, Amasai, Zechariah, Benaiah, and Eliezer, the priests, were to blow the trumpets before the ark of God. Obed-edom and Jehiah also were to be gatekeepers for the ark.

6:12–19a

No parallel

15:25—16:3

16 ⁴He appointed certain of the Levites as ministers before the ark of the LORD, to invoke, to thank, and to praise the LORD, the God of Israel. ⁵Asaph was the chief, and second to him Zechariah, Jeiel, Shemiramoth, Jehiel, Mattithiah, Eliab, Benaiah, Obed-edom, and Jeiel, with harps and lyres; Asaph was to sound the cymbals, ⁶and the priests Benaiah and Jahaziel were to blow trumpets regularly, before the ark of the covenant of God. ⁷Then on that day David first appointed the singing of praises to the LORD by Asaph and his kindred

2 Samuel 6:1-23

6 ¹⁹ᵇThen all the people went back to their homes. ²⁰ David returned to bless his household. But Michal the daughter of Saul came out to meet David, and said, "How the king of Israel honored himself today, uncovering himself today before the eyes of his servants' maids, as any vulgar fellow might shamelessly uncover himself!" ²¹David said to Michal, "It was before the LORD, who chose me in place of your father and all his household, to appoint me as prince over Israel, the people of the LORD, that I have danced before the LORD. ²²I will make myself yet more contemptible than this, and I will be abased in my own eyes; but by the maids of whom you have spoken, by them I shall be held in honor." ²³And Michal the daughter of Saul had no child to the day of her death

1 Chronicles 13:–16:7

No parallel

14. After the Exile: Overview

THE CHRONICLER'S HISTORY

Date: ca. 400 BC

Situation: Writing in post-exilic Judah, the Chronicler reinterpreted the Deuteronomistic History to meet the needs of his community.

Themes:
- All Israel invited to worship in Jerusalem if they return to the LORD (1 Chr 11:1–3; 2 Chr 1:2; 30:1, 5–9; 31:1)
- Idealized memories:
  - David portrayed as the founder of the temple cult
  - David's role with regard to worship stressed
  - Negative portrayals of David and Solomon in the Deuteronomistic History eliminated
- Immediate retribution rather than intergenerational punishment (2 Chr 33:10–13; 2 Chr 35:21–22)
- Levites' role in worship stressed (1 Chr 15:16–24; 16:4–42; 28:21; 2 Chr 29:18)
- Temple construction and worship central to the Chronicler's history (1 Chr 22; 1 Chr 28:1–29:9; 2 Chr 2:1–7:11; 2 Chr 29:3–26)

JOEL

Date: ca. 400 BC

Situation: Faced with a plague of locusts, a scorching desert wind, or an enemy invasion, Joel calls for repentance. The people's repentance leads to a promise of blessing and hope.

Themes:
- Day of the LORD:
  - Impending judgment affecting the whole community coupled with a call for repentant fasting and prayer (Joel 1:2—2:17)
  - Promise of restoration, outpouring of the spirit (Joel 2:18—3:1 [2:18—4:1 NAB and NJB]; 3:17–21 [4:17–21 NAB and NJB])
  - Judgment against the nations (Joel 3:2–16 [4:2–16 NAB and NJB])

MALACHI

Date: ca. mid-fifth century BC

Situation: Malachi, "my messenger," addressed the liturgical and social abuses that arose after the temple was rebuilt.

Structure: The author uses a series of teaching dialogues, each of which includes a statement, question, and response.

Themes:
- Abuses:
  - Liturgical, in particular priestly corruption (Mal 1:6—2:9)
  - Marriage to foreign women and divorce (Mal 2:10-17)
- Coming of Elijah (Mal 4:5 [3:23 NAB and NJB])
- Day of the LORD, judgment for evildoers and salvation for the righteous (Mal 3:1—4:5 [3:1-24 NAB and NJB])

DEUTERO-ZECHARIAH (ZECHARIAH 9–14)

Date: Uncertain, possibly fourth century BC

Structure: Two oracles: Zechariah 9–11 and 12–14

Themes:
- Day of the LORD (Zech 12:2—14:21)
- False shepherds have mistreated the people and will be punished (Zech 10:3; 11:4-17)
- Image of God as warrior/redeemer (Zech 9:1-17; 10:3-5; 14:12-15)
- Messianic hope for a king who will bring peace (Zech 9:9-10)

RUTH

Date: Uncertain

Situation: God's providence is seen at work in the story of two widows in a patriarchal society during the time of the Judges. David's ancestry is traced to the foreigner, Ruth.

Literary Style: Short story

Themes:
- Covenant fidelity/loyalty; relationship of Ruth and Naomi as a sign of God's covenant loyalty and love (Ruth 1:14-21; 2:11; 3:10-11; 4:15b)
- God's providence (Ruth 1:6-9; 2:3, 12, 20; 4:12-15)
- Openness to foreigners (Ruth 1:22; 2:6, 10, 12)

SONG OF SOLOMON (SONG OF SONGS)

Date: A post-exilic collection with ancient roots

Literary Style: Collection of love songs using rich sensual imagery

Theme:
- Celebration of love:
  - Human love
  - Allegory of the relationship between God and the community
  - Allegory of the relationship between God and the individual

PSALMS

Date: A post-exilic collection with ancient roots

Situation: Liturgical songs that were used in the second temple

Literary Style: Hebrew poetry using antithetic, synonymous, and other types of parallelism

Theme: Prayerful response to God in a wide range of situations

Categories/types:
- Supplication and lament, communal and individual
- Confidence
- Thanksgiving, communal and individual
- Praise
- Historical narrative
- Royal/messianic
- Prophetic
- Wisdom

15. Synoptic Comparison 2: Solomon's Prayer

1 Kings 8:54–62

⁵⁴Now as Solomon finished offering all this prayer and this plea to the LORD, he arose from facing the altar of the LORD, where he had knelt with hands outstretched toward heaven; ⁵⁵he stood and blessed all the assembly of Israel with a loud voice:

⁵⁶"Blessed be the LORD, who has given rest to his people Israel according to all that he promised; not one word has failed of all his good promise, which he spoke through his servant Moses. ⁵⁷The LORD our God be with us, as he was with our ancestors; may he not leave us or abandon us, ⁵⁸but incline our hearts to him, to walk in all his ways, and to keep his commandments, his statutes, and his ordinances, which he commanded our ancestors. ⁵⁹Let these words of mine, with which I pleaded before the LORD, be near to the LORD our God day and night, and may he maintain the cause of his servant and the cause of his people Israel, as each day requires; ⁶⁰so that all the peoples of the earth may know that the LORD is God; there is no other. ⁶¹Therefore devote yourselves completely to the LORD our God, walking in his statutes and keeping his commandments, as at this day."

2 Chronicles 7:1–4

¹When Solomon ended his prayer,

Fire came down from heaven and consumed the burnt offering and the sacrifices; and the glory of the LORD filled the temple. ²The priests could not enter the house of the LORD, because the glory of the LORD filled the LORD's house. ³When all the people of Israel saw the fire come down and the glory of the LORD on the temple, they bowed down on the pavement with their faces to the

ground, and worshiped and gave thanks to the LORD, saying,
"For he is good,
for his steadfast love endures forever."

62Then the king, and all Israel with him, offered sacrifices before the LORD.

4Then the king and all the people offered sacrifice before the LORD.

16. The Prayer of Manasseh

(An Apocryphal Prayer of King Manasseh Mentioned in 2 Chronicles 33:18–19)

Ascription of Praise

[1]O Lord Almighty,
God of our ancestors,
of Abraham and Isaac and Jacob
and of their righteous offspring;
[2]you who made heaven and earth
with all their order;
[3]who shackled the sea by your word of command,
who confined the deep
and sealed it with your terrible and glorious name;
[4]at whom all things shudder,
and tremble before your power,
[5]for your glorious splendor cannot be borne,
and the wrath of your threat to sinners is unendurable;
[6]yet immeasurable and unsearchable
is your promised mercy,
[7]for you are the Lord Most High,
of great compassion, long-suffering, and very merciful,
and you relent at human suffering.
O Lord, according to your great goodness
you have promised repentance and forgiveness
to those who have sinned against you,
and in the multitude of your mercies
you have appointed repentance for sinners,
so that they may be saved.
[8]Therefore you, O Lord, God of the righteous,
have not appointed repentance for the righteous,
for Abraham and Isaac and Jacob, who did not sin against you,
but you have appointed repentance for me, who am a sinner.

Confession of Sins

[9]For the sins I have committed are more in number than the sand of the sea;
my transgressions are multiplied, O Lord, they are multiplied!
I am not worthy to look up and see the height of heaven
because of the multitude of my iniquities.

[10]I am weighted down with many an iron fetter,
so that I am rejected because of my sins,
and I have no relief;

    for I have provoked your wrath
    and have done what is evil in your sight,
    setting up abominations and multiplying offenses.

Supplication for Pardon

[11]And now I bend the knee of my heart,
imploring you for your kindness.
[12]I have sinned, O Lord, I have sinned,
and I acknowledge my transgressions.
[13]I earnestly implore you,
forgive me, O Lord, forgive me!
Do not destroy me with my transgressions!
Do not be angry with me for ever or store up evil for me;
do not condemn me to the depths of the earth.
For you, O Lord, are the God of those who repent,
[14]and in me you will manifest your goodness;
for, unworthy as I am, you will save me according to your great mercy,
[15]and I will praise you continually all the days of my life.
For all the host of heaven sings your praise,
and yours is the glory for ever. Amen.

(Prayer of Manasseh 1–15; NRSV)

17. Self-Quiz: Mid-Unit Three

Match the following statements with the appropriate book (a book may be used more than once):

_____ 1. Story of ancestor of David

_____ 2. Locust plague as a sign
   of the Day of the LORD

_____ 3. Idealized David

_____ 4. Promised the return of Elijah

_____ 5. Celebration of human and divine love

_____ 6. Re-interpretation of history to meet the needs
   of the post-exilic community

_____ 7. Saw the outpouring of the spirit as one of the signs
   of the Day of the LORD

_____ 8. Title of the book means "my messenger"

_____ 9. Often interpreted in an allegorical way by both
   Jews and Christians

_____ 10. Stressed immediate retribution

_____ 11. Used teaching dialogues

_____ 12. Very open to foreigners

_____ 13. Focused on the importance of ritual and temple worship
   and the role of the Levites

_____ 14. Announced a king coming into Jerusalem on a donkey

_____ 15. Story of God's providence

a. Chronicles

b. Malachi ·

c. Joel ·

d. Deutero-Zechariah

e. Ruth

f. Song of Solomon
   (Song of Songs)

(Answers to quiz can be found on page 105.)

18. Types of Psalms

Carroll Stuhlmueller, CP

OUTLINE OF PSALMS ACCORDING TO LITERARY FORM

HYMNS OF PRAISE

Motivation from Nature:
Psalms 8, 19:1-7, 29, 33, 89:1-19, 93, 96, 104, 148, 150

Motivation from History or Torah:
Psalms 19:8-14, 24, 33, 46, 47, 48, 68, 76, 78, 100, 105, 107, 113, 114, 117, 134, 135, 136, 145, 146, 147, 149, 150

Yahweh-King:
Psalms 24, 29, 47, 93, 95:1-7a, 96, 97, 98, 99, 149

Canticles of Zion:
Psalms 46, 48, 76, 84, 87, 122

Entrance or Processional Liturgies:
Psalms 15, 24, 68, 95:1-7a, 100, 132

PRAYERS OF SUPPLICATION AND LAMENT

For the Assembly:
Psalms 12, 36, 44, 53, 58, 60, 74, 79, 80, 83, 85, 90, 94, 106, 108:7-14, 137, 144:1-11

For the Individual:
Psalms 3, 4, 5, 6, 7, 9-10, 13, 14, 17, 22, 25, 26, 27, 28, 35, 38, 39, 40:14-18, 41, 42-43, 51, 53, 54, 55, 56, 57, 59, 61, 63, 64, 69, 70, 71, 86, 88, 102, 108:2-6, 109, 120, 123, 130, 139, 140, 141, 142, 143

For the Sick:
Psalms 6, 16, 30, 31, 38, 39, 41, 69, 88, 91, 103

Seven Penitential Psalms:
Psalms 6, 32, 38, 51, 102, 130, 143

Curse Psalms:
Psalms 10:15, 31:17-18, 40:15, 55:15, 58:6-11, 59:10-13, 68:22-23, 69:22-28, 83:9-18, 109:6-20, 137:9, 139:18-21, 140:8-10

THANKSGIVING PSALMS

For the Assembly:
Psalms 22:22-31, 34, 65, 66, 67, 68, 75, 76, 92, 107, 118, 122, 124, 135, 136

For the Individual:
Psalms 18, 23, 30, 31, 40:2-12, 63, 66, 103, 116, 118:5-21, 138, 144:1-11

PRAYERS OF CONFIDENCE

Psalms 11, 16, 20, 23, 27, 41, 52, 62, 63, 84, 91, 115, 121, 125, 126, 129, 131, 133

WISDOM PSALMS

Psalms 1, 25, 32, 34, 36, 37, 49, 62, 73, 75, 78, 111, 112, 119, 127, 128

Alphabetic or Acrostic:
> Psalms 9–10, 25, 34, 37, 111, 112, 119, 146

ROYAL DAVIDIC PSALMS

Coronation or Anniversary:
> Psalms 2, 72, 89:1–37, 101, 110, 132

Supplication:
> Psalms 20, 21, 61, 89, 144:1–11

Marriage:
> Psalm 45

Thanksgiving:
> Psalm 18

PROPHETIC PSALMS

> Psalms 50, 81, 82, 95:7b–11

Carroll Stuhlmueller, CP, *Psalms (Psalms 1–72)* (Wilmington: Michael Glazier, 1983), 53–55.

19. Rereadings (Relectures)

Excerpt from *The Interpretation of the Bible in the Church*, §III. A. 1.

One thing that gives the Bible an inner unity, unique of its kind, is the fact that later biblical writings often depend upon earlier ones. These more recent writings allude to older ones, create "rereadings" (relectures) which develop new aspects of meaning, sometimes quite different from the original sense. A text may also make explicit reference to older passages, whether it is to deepen their meaning or to make known their fulfillment.

Thus it is that the inheritance of the land, promised by God to Abraham for his offspring (Gen 15:7,18), becomes entrance into the sanctuary of God (Exod 15:17), a participation in God's "rest" (Ps 132:7-8) reserved for those who truly have faith (Ps 95:8-11; Heb 3:7—4:11) and, finally, entrance into the heavenly sanctuary (Heb 6:12, 18-20), "the eternal inheritance" (Heb 9:15).

The prophecy of Nathan, which promised David a "house," that is a dynastic succession, "secure forever" (2 Sam 7:12-16), is recalled in a number of rephrasings (2 Sam 23:5; 1 Kgs 2:4; 3:6; 1 Chr 17:11-14), arising especially out of times of distress (Ps 89:20-38), not without significant changes; it is continued by other prophecies (Ps 2:7-8; 110:1, 4; Amos 9:11; Isa 7:13-14; Jer 23:56, etc.), some of which announce the return of the kingdom of David itself (Hos 3:5; Jer 30:9; Ezek 34:24; 37:24-25; cf. Mark 11:10). The promised kingdom becomes universal (Ps 2:8; Dan 2:35, 44; 7:14; cf. Matt 28:18). It brings to fullness the vocation of human beings (Gen 1:28; Ps 8:6-9; Wis 9:2-3; 10:2).

The prophecy of Jeremiah concerning the 70 years of chastisement incurred by Jerusalem and Judah (Jer 25:11-12; 29:10) is recalled in 2 Chr 25:20-23 which affirms that this punishment has actually occurred. Nonetheless, much later, the author of Daniel returns to reflect upon it once more, convinced that this word of God still conceals a hidden meaning that could throw light upon the situation of his own day (Dan 9:24-27).

The basic affirmation of the retributive justice of God, rewarding the good and punishing the evil (Ps 1:1-6; 112:1-10; Lev 26:3-33; etc.), flies in the face of much immediate experience, which often fails to bear it out. In the face of this, Scripture allows strong voices of protestation and argument to be heard (Ps 44; Job 10:1-7; 13:3-28; 23-24), as little by little it plumbs more profoundly the full depths of the mystery (Ps 37; Job 38-42; Isa 53; Wis 3-5).

Pontifical Biblical Commission, *The Interpretation of the Bible in the Church*, 1993, III, A, 1.

20. Self-Quiz: Unit Three Maps

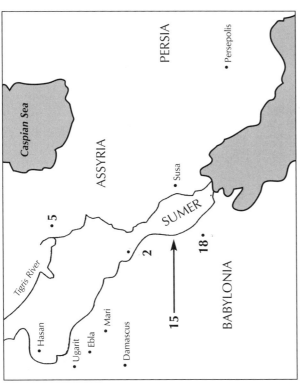

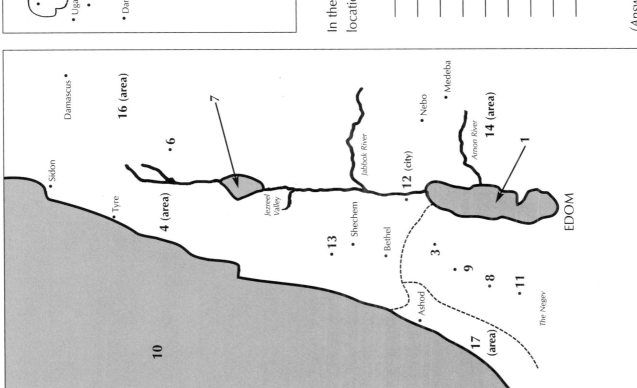

In the blank before each place name, write the number of the location on the maps.

_____ a. Babylon

_____ b. Beersheba

_____ c. Bethlehem

_____ d. Dan

_____ e. Dead Sea

_____ f. Euphrates River

_____ g. Hebron

_____ h. Jericho

_____ i. Jerusalem

_____ j. Mediterranean Sea

_____ k. Moab

_____ l. Nineveh

_____ m. Philistia

_____ n. Phoenicia

_____ o. Samaria (city)

_____ p. Sea of Galilee

_____ q. Syria

_____ r. Ur

(Answers to quiz can be found on page 105.)

Self-Quiz Answers

Answers to Self-Quiz
Mid-Unit One
1. b
2. c
3. c
4. d
5. c
6. c
7. b
8. f
9. e
10. a
11. d
12. b

Answers to Self-Quiz
Unit One Maps
a. 6
b. 3
c. 1
d. 2
e. 5
f. 4

Answers to Self-Quiz
Mid-Unit Two
1. d
2. a
3. d
4. c
5. d
6. d
7. c
8. b
9. e or f
10. a
11. c
12. d
13. d
14. e
15. f

Answers to Self-Quiz
Unit Two Map
a. 6
b. 3
c. 7
d. 5
e. 2
f. 4
g. 1

Answers to Self-Quiz
Mid-Unit Three
1. e
2. c
3. a
4. b
5. f
6. a
7. c
8. b
9. f
10. a
11. b
12. e
13. a
14. d
15. e

Answers to Self-Quiz
Unit Three Maps
a. 2
b. 11
c. 9
d. 6
e. 1
f. 15
g. 8
h. 12
i. 3
j. 10
k. 14
l. 5
m. 17
n. 4
o. 13
p. 7
q. 16
r. 18

FOUR-YEAR PLAN OF STUDY IN THE CATHOLIC BIBLICAL SCHOOL

UNITS	BIBLICAL BOOKS	THEOLOGICAL THEMES	GENERAL ISSUES
FIRST YEAR: OLD TESTAMENT FOUNDATIONS — GENESIS THROUGH KINGS			
UNIT 1	Exodus Leviticus Numbers	People of God Covenant Desert	Sources of the Pentateuch
UNIT 2	Deuteronomy Genesis	Promise/The Land Creation/Sin	Form Criticism Fertile Crescent
UNIT 3	Joshua Judges 1 and 2 Samuel 1 and 2 Kings	Charismatic Leadership Kingship Prophecy	Geography of Palestine Canaanite Religion Biblical Chronology Biblical Archeology
SECOND YEAR: NEW TESTAMENT FOUNDATIONS — JESUS AND DISCIPLESHIP			
UNIT 1	Mark Luke Matthew 1 and 2	Discipleship Holy Spirit Infancy Narratives	Synoptic Question Form Criticism Redaction Criticism
UNIT 2	Acts Pauline Letters	Church Gifts of the Holy Spirit	New Testament Geography Letter as Literary Form
UNIT 3	John and Johannine Letters Mark 13, Luke 21 Matthew 24—25 Revelation	Sacraments Eschatology	Apocalyptic Writing
THIRD YEAR: OLD TESTAMENT CONTINUED — EXILE AND RESTORATION			
UNIT 1	Amos Hosea 1 Isaiah Micah Zephaniah Nahum Jeremiah	Social Justice Prophetic Vocation Marriage of God and Israel	Biblical Chronology
UNIT 2	Lamentations Obadiah Ezekiel 2 Isaiah Haggai Zechariah 1—8 3 Isaiah Ezra Nehemiah	Destruction of the Temple Meaning of the Exile Renewal after Exile Community Rebuilt around the Word	Crisis of the Exile Strategies of Renewal
UNIT 3	1 and 2 Chronicles Joel Malachi Zechariah 9–14 Ruth Song of Songs Psalms	Rebuilding a People Importance of the Law	Historical Writings of Old Testament Hebrew Poetry Jewish Liturgy
FOURTH YEAR: BOTH TESTAMENTS CONCLUDED — THE WORD IN THE HELLENISTIC WORLD			
UNIT 1	Proverbs Habakkuk Job Ecclesiastes Sirach Wisdom	Creation Emphasis Problem of Suffering	Priest, Prophet, and Sage
UNIT 2	Jonah Esther Tobit Baruch 1 and 2 Maccabees Judith Daniel	 Martyrdom Resurrection	Deuterocanonical Books Hellenism
UNIT 3	Matthew Pastoral Letters Catholic Letters Hebrews	Role of Peter/Apostles New Testament as Fulfillment of Old Testament	Christianity as a New Form of Religion in the Roman World